CHOOSE
HIGHER
GROUND

CHOOSE
HIGHER
GROUND

HENRY B. EYRING

DESERET
BOOK

Salt Lake City, Utah

© 2013 Henry B. Eyring

DESERET BOOK is a registered trademark of Deseret Book Company.

Visit us at DeseretBook.com

Library of Congress Cataloging-in-Publication Data

(CIP on file)
ISBN 978-1-60907-463-0

Printed in the United States of America
Edwards Brothers Malloy, Ann Arbor, MI

10 9 8 7 6 5 4 3 2 1

CONTENTS

Contents

A STRONG
FOUNDATION

THIS DAY

There is a danger in the word *someday* when what it means is "not this day." "Someday I will repent." "Someday I will forgive him." "Someday I will speak to my friend about the Church." "Someday I will start to pay tithing." "Someday I will return to the temple." "Someday . . ."

The scriptures make the danger of delay clear. It is that we may discover that we have run out of time. The God who gives us each day as a treasure will require an accounting. We will weep, and He will weep, if we have intended to repent and to serve Him in tomorrows which never came or have dreamt of yesterdays where the opportunity to act was past. This day is a precious gift of God. The thought "Someday I will" can be a thief of the opportunities of time and the blessings of eternity.

There is solemn warning and counsel in the words recorded in the Book of Mormon:

> *The thought "Someday I will" can be a thief of the opportunities of time and the blessings of eternity.*

"And now, as I said unto you before, as ye have had so many witnesses, therefore, I beseech of you that ye do not procrastinate the day of your repentance until the end; for after this day of life,

3

which is given us to prepare for eternity, behold, if we do not improve our time while in this life, then cometh the night of darkness
wherein there can be no labor performed.

"Ye cannot say, when ye are brought to that awful crisis, that I
will repent, that I will return to my God. Nay, ye cannot say this;
for that same spirit which doth possess your bodies at the time that
ye go out of this life, that same spirit will have power to possess
your body in that eternal world" (Alma 34:33–34).

Then Amulek warns that procrastinating your repentance and
service can cause the Spirit of the Lord to withdraw from you. But
with the warning he gives this hope: "And this I know, because the
Lord hath said he dwelleth not in unholy temples, but in the hearts
of the righteous doth he dwell; yea, and he has also said that the
righteous shall sit down in his kingdom, to go no more out; but
their garments should be made white through the blood of the
Lamb" (Alma 34:36).

The scriptures are filled with examples of wise servants of God
who treasured the day they were in and chose to do what they
could to bring cleansing. Joshua was one: "Choose you this day
whom ye will serve . . . ," he said, "but as for me and my house, we
will serve the Lord" (Joshua 24:15).

Serving Him invites the Holy Ghost to be with us. And the
Holy Ghost is a cleanser of sin.

Even the Savior, who was without sin, set an example of the
need not to procrastinate. He said:

"I must work the works of him that sent me, while it is day:
the night cometh, when no man can work.

"As long as I am in the world, I am the light of the world"
(John 9:4–5).

As the risen Savior, He is this day and forever the Light of the
World. It is He who invites us to come unto Him and serve Him,

without delay. His encouragement to you and to me is this: "I love them that love me; and those that seek me early shall find me" (Proverbs 8:17).

That is as true of a day as it is of a life. A morning prayer and an early search in the scriptures to know what we should do for the Lord can set the course of a day. We can know which task, of all those we might choose, matters most to God and therefore to us. I have learned such a prayer is always answered if we ask and ponder with childlike submission, ready to act without delay to perform even the most humble service.

A morning prayer and an early search in the scriptures to know what we should do for the Lord can set the course of a day.

On many days, doing what matters most will not be easy. It is not supposed to be. God's purpose in creation was to let us prove ourselves. The plan was explained to us in the spirit world before we were born. We were valiant enough there to qualify for the opportunity to choose against temptation here to prepare for eternal life, the greatest of all the gifts of God. We rejoiced to know the test would be one of faithful obedience even when it would not be easy.

Hard as we knew the test would be, we felt joy because we had confidence that we could pass it. Our confidence came from knowing that Jesus Christ would come into the world as our Savior. He would overcome death. He would make it possible for us to be cleansed of our sins by qualifying for the effects of His Atonement.

We also knew some reassuring facts about what it would take to receive the purifying which we would need. Everything that cleansing would require—baptism by authority, receiving the Holy

Ghost under the hands of authorized priesthood bearers, remembering Him and therefore having His Spirit to be with us, and then keeping His commandments—all would be possible for the humblest of us. It would not take superior intellect, nor would it take wealth, nor long life. And we knew that the Savior would draw us to Him and would have the power to help us when the test would be hard and the temptation to procrastinate great.

All of us will need His help to avoid the tragedy of procrastinating what we must do here and now to have eternal life. For most of us the temptation to delay will come from one or both of two feelings. They are polar opposites: one is to be complacent about what we have already done, and the other is to feel overwhelmed by the need to do more.

Complacency is a danger for us all. It can come to naive youth who feel that there will be plenty of time in the future for spiritual things. They might think that they have already done enough, considering the brief time they have lived. I know from experience how the Lord can help such a youth to see that he or she is in the midst of spiritual things, now. He can help you see that classmates are watching you. He can help you see that their eternal future is shaped by what they observe you do or not do. Your simple thanks for their influence for good on you can lift them more than you imagine. When you ask God, He can and will reveal to you the opportunities to lift others for Him, which He has placed around you from your infancy.

Complacency can affect even the seasoned adult. The better and the longer you serve, the more likely that the tempter can place this lie in your mind: "You have earned a rest." You may have been the Primary president in your little branch twice. Or you may have worked long and hard on your mission and sacrificed so much to serve. Or perhaps you were the pioneer in the Church where you live. The thought may come: "Why not leave the service to the new people. I have done my part." The temptation will be to believe that you will return to serve again, someday.

The Lord can help you see the danger in taking a rest because you feel you have done enough. He helped me by letting me have a conversation with one of His aged servants. He was feeble, his body weakened by decades of faithful labor and by illness. His doctors no longer allowed him to leave his home. At his request, I reported a trip I had taken in the Lord's service, across several nations, in dozens of meetings, and in many private interviews, helping individuals and families. I told him of the gratitude people expressed to me for him and his many years of service. He asked me if I had another assignment soon. I told him about another long trip soon to come. He surprised me, and he gave me an inoculation against complacency which I hope will last forever, when he grabbed my arm and said, "Oh, please, take me with you."

When you ask God, He can and will reveal to you the opportunities to lift others for Him, which He has placed around you from your infancy.

It is hard to know when we have done enough for the Atonement to change our natures and so qualify us for eternal life. And we don't know how many days we will have to give the service necessary for that mighty change to come. But we know that we will have days enough if only we don't waste them. Here is the good news:

"And the days of the children of men were prolonged,

according to the will of God, that they might repent while in the flesh; wherefore, their state became a state of probation, and their time was lengthened, according to the commandments which the Lord God gave unto the children of men" (2 Nephi 2:21).

That assurance from the Master can help those of us feeling overwhelmed by our circumstances. In the hardest trials, as long as you have the power to pray, you can ask a loving God: "Please let me serve, this day. It doesn't matter to me how few things I may be able to do. Just let me know what I *can* do. I will obey this day. I know that I can, with Thy help."

The quiet invitation to you may be to do so simple a thing as to forgive someone who has offended you. You can do that from a hospital bed. It may be to go to help someone who is hungry. You may feel overwhelmed by your own poverty and the labors of the day. But if you decide not to wait until you have more strength and more money, and if you pray for the Holy Spirit as you go, you will when you arrive know what to do and how to help someone even poorer than you are. You may find when you get there that they were praying and expecting that someone like you would come, in the name of the Lord.

For those who are discouraged by their circumstances and are therefore tempted to feel they cannot serve the Lord this day, I make you two promises. Hard as things seem today, they will be better in the next day if you choose to serve the Lord this day with your whole heart. Your circumstances may not be improved in all the ways which you desire. But you will have been given new strength to carry your burdens and new confidence that when your burdens become too heavy, the Lord, whom you have served, will carry what you cannot. He knows how. He prepared long ago. He suffered your infirmities and your sorrows when He was in the flesh so that He would know how to succor you.

The other promise I make to you is that by choosing to serve Him this day, you will feel His love and grow to love Him more. You may remember the scripture:

"I say unto you, I would that ye should remember to retain the name written always in your hearts . . . that ye hear and know the voice by which ye shall be called, and also, the name by which he shall call you.

"For how knoweth a man the master whom he has not served, and who is a stranger unto him, and is far from the thoughts and intents of his heart?" (Mosiah 5:12–13).

By serving Him this day, you will come to know Him better. You will feel His love and appreciation. You would not want

If you decide not to wait until you have more strength and more money, and if you pray for the Holy Spirit as you go, you will when you arrive know what to do and how to help someone.

to delay receiving that blessing. And feeling His love will draw you back to His service, wiping away both complacency and discouragement.

Help Them on Their Way Home

Our Heavenly Father wants and needs our help to bring His spirit children home to Him again. This includes young people who are already within His true Church and so are started on the strait and narrow way to return to their heavenly home. He wants them to gain early the spiritual strength to stay on the path. And He needs our help to get them back to the path quickly should they begin to wander.

I was a young bishop when I began to see clearly why the Lord wants us to strengthen children when they are young and rescue them quickly. I will tell you one story of a young person who represents many whom I have tried to help over the years.

She sat across from me at my bishop's desk. She spoke to me of her life. She had been baptized and confirmed as a member of the Church when she was eight. There were no tears in her eyes as she recounted the more than twenty years that followed, but there was sadness in her voice. She said that the downward spiral began with choices to associate with what she thought were exciting people. She began to violate what at first seemed to be less important commandments.

She felt at first a little sadness and a twinge of guilt. But the associations with her friends provided a new feeling of being liked, and so her occasional resolutions to repent seemed less and less important. As the gravity of the commandments she was breaking increased, the dream of a happy eternal home seemed to fade.

She sat across from me in what she called misery. She wanted me to rescue her from the trap of sin in which she found herself bound. But the only way out was for her to exercise faith in Jesus Christ, to have a broken heart, to repent, and so be cleansed, changed, and strengthened through the Lord's Atonement. I bore my testimony to her that it was still possible. And it was, but so much harder than it would have been to exercise faith early in her life on the journey home to God and when she first began to wander.

So we help God's children best by providing ways to build faith in Jesus Christ and His

We help God's children best by providing ways to build faith in Jesus Christ and His restored gospel when they are young. And then we must help rekindle that faith quickly before it dims as they wander off the path.

restored gospel when they are young. And then we must help rekindle that faith quickly before it dims as they wander off the path.

So you and I can expect a nearly continuous opportunity to help travelers among God's children. The Savior told us why that would be so when He described the perilous journey home for all of God's spirit children through the mists which sin and Satan create:

"Enter ye in at the strait gate; for wide is the gate, and broad is the way, which leadeth to destruction, and many there be who go in thereat;

"Because strait is the gate, and narrow is the way, which leadeth unto life, and few there be that find it" (3 Nephi 14:13–14).

Foreseeing the needs of His children, a loving Heavenly Father placed directions and rescuers along their way. He sent His Son, Jesus Christ, to make safe passage possible and visible. He called prophets to teach us not only how to stay on the path but also how to rescue those who have been led away into sorrow.

Heavenly Father has assigned us to a great variety of stations to strengthen and, when needed, to lead travelers to safety. Our most important and powerful assignments are in the family. They are important because the family has the opportunity at the start of a child's life to put feet firmly on the path home. Parents, brothers and sisters, grandparents, aunts and uncles are made more powerful guides and rescuers by the bonds of love that are the very nature of a family.

The family has an advantage in the first eight years of a child's life. In those protected years, because of the Atonement of Jesus Christ, Satan's use of the mists of darkness to hide the path to return home is blocked. In those precious years the Lord helps families by calling Primary workers to help strengthen children spiritually. He also provides holders of the Aaronic Priesthood to offer the sacrament. In those sacramental prayers, the children hear the promise that they may someday receive the Holy Ghost as a guide if they are obedient to God's commandments. As a result, they are fortified to resist temptation when it comes and then, sometime in the future, to go to the rescue of others.

Many bishops in the Church are inspired to call the strongest people in the ward to serve individual children in the Primary. They realize that if the children are strengthened with faith and testimony, they will be less likely to need rescue as teenagers. They realize that a strong spiritual foundation can make the difference for a lifetime.

We all can help. Grandmothers, grandfathers, and every member who knows a child can help. It doesn't take a formal calling in Primary. Nor is it limited by age. One such woman, as a younger person, was on the Primary general board that helped create the CTR motto.

She never tired of serving the children. She taught in the Primary of her ward, at her own request, until she was almost 90 years old. Little children could feel her love for them. They saw her example. They learned from her the simple principles of the gospel of Jesus Christ. And above all, because of her example they learned to feel and recognize the Holy Ghost. And when they did, they were well on their way to the faith to resist temptation. They would be less likely to need to be rescued and would be prepared to go to the rescue of others.

I learned the power of simple faith in prayer and in the Holy Ghost when our children were small. Our oldest son was not yet baptized. His parents, Primary teachers, and priesthood servants had tried to help him feel and recognize the Spirit and know how to receive His help.

One afternoon my wife had taken him to the home of a woman who was teaching him to read. Our plan was that I was to pick him up on my way home from work.

His lesson ended earlier than we had expected. He felt confident that he knew the way home. So he started to walk. He said afterward that he had complete confidence and liked the idea of being alone on the trip. After he had gone about half a mile, it started to grow dark. He began to sense that he was still very far from home.

He can still remember that the lights of the cars as they streamed past him were blurred by his tears. He felt like a little child, not the confident boy who had begun to walk home alone. He realized that he needed help. Then something came to his memory. He knew he was supposed to pray. And so he left the road and headed toward some trees he could barely see in the darkness. He found a place to kneel down.

Through the bushes he could hear voices coming toward him. Two young people had heard him crying. As they approached, they said, "Can we help you?" Through his tears he told them he was lost and that he wanted to go home. They asked if he knew his home phone number or address. He didn't. They asked if he knew his name. He did know that. They led him to the nearby place where they lived. They found our family name in a phone book.

When I got the phone call, I rushed to the rescue, grateful that kind people had been placed along his way home. And I have been ever grateful he was taught to pray with faith that help would come when he was lost. That faith has led him to safety and brought him more rescuers more times than he can count.

The Lord has placed a pattern of rescue and rescuers in His kingdom. In His wisdom the Lord has inspired His servants to place some of the most powerful ways to strengthen us and to put in place the best rescuers as we pass through the teenage years.

You know of two powerful programs provided by the Lord. One, for young women, is called Personal Progress. The other, for Aaronic Priesthood holders, is called Duty to God. We encourage young people in the rising generation to see their own potential to build great spiritual strength. And we plead with those who care about those young people to rise to what the Lord requires of us to help them. And since the future of the Church depends upon them, all of us care.

The two programs have been improved, but their purpose remains unchanged. President Thomas S. Monson put it this way: we must "learn what we should learn, do what we should do, and be what we should be" ("To Learn, to Do, to Be," *Ensign,* November 2008, 67).

The *Personal Progress* booklet for young women makes the purpose clear for them: "The Personal Progress program uses the eight Young Women values to help you under-

> *The Lord has placed a pattern of rescue and rescuers in His kingdom.*

stand more fully who you are, why you are here on the earth, and what you should be doing as a daughter of God to prepare for the day you go to the temple to make sacred covenants."

It goes on to say that young women will "make commitments, carry them out, and report your progress to a parent or leader." It also promises that "the patterns you establish as you work on Personal Progress—such as prayer, scripture study, service, and journal keeping—will become personal daily habits. These habits will strengthen your testimony and help you learn and improve throughout your life." (*Young Women Personal Progess* [booklet, 2009], 6).

The Duty to God program for young men in the Aaronic Priesthood is another powerful tool. It will strengthen the testimonies of young men and their relationship with God. It will help them learn and want to fulfill their priesthood duties. It will strengthen their relationships with their parents, among quorum members, and with their leaders.

Both of these programs put great responsibility on the efforts of the young people themselves. They are invited to learn and do things that would be challenging for anyone. As I reflect on my own youth, I cannot remember being so challenged. Oh, on a few occasions I was invited to rise to such tests, but only now and then. These programs expect consistency, great effort, and the accumulation of learning and spiritual experiences over years.

On reflection I realized that the contents of these booklets are a physical representation of the Lord's trust in the rising generation and in all of us who love them. And I have seen evidence that the trust is well placed.

In visits I watched Aaronic Priesthood quorums in action. I have seen young men following patterns of learning, making plans to do what God wants of them, then moving out to do what they have committed to do and sharing with others how they were changed spiritually. And as I watched and listened, it became clear that fathers, mothers, leaders, friends, and even neighbors in a congregation were touched by the Spirit as they heard youth testify how they had been strengthened. The youth were lifted as they bore testimony, and so were those who were trying to help them rise.

The Young Women program has in it that same powerful pattern to develop spiritual strength in the young women and to offer the opportunity for us to help. Personal Progress helps young women prepare to receive the ordinances of the temple. They are helped by the examples of mothers, grandmothers, and every righteous woman around them in the Church. I have seen how parents helped a daughter achieve her goals and dreams by noticing and appreciating all the good things she does. I have watched a mother stand with her young daughter as they received recognition for having together become examples of outstanding womanhood. And as they shared with me what it had meant to them, I felt the Lord's approval and encouragement for us all.

Of all the help we can give these young people, the greatest will be to let them feel our confidence that they are on the path home to God and that they can make it. And we do that best by going with them. Because the path is steep and sometimes rocky, they will at times feel discouraged and even stumble. They may at times become confused about their destination and wander after less eternally important goals. These inspired programs make that less likely because they will lead the young person to invite and receive the companionship of the Holy Ghost.

> *Of all the help we can give these young people, the greatest will be to let them feel our confidence that they are on the path home to God and that they can make it. And we do that best by going with them.*

The best counsel for us to give young people is that they can arrive back to Heavenly Father only as they are guided and corrected by the Spirit of God. So if we are wise, we will encourage, praise, and exemplify everything which invites the companionship of the Holy Ghost. When they share with us what they are doing and feeling, we must ourselves have qualified for the Spirit. Then they will feel in our praise and our smiles the approval of God. And should we feel the need to give corrective counsel, they will feel our love and the love of God in it, not rebuke and rejection, which can permit Satan to lead them further away.

The example they most need from us is to do what they must do. We need to pray for the gifts of the Spirit. We need to ponder in the scriptures and in the words of living prophets. We need to make plans which are not only wishes but covenants. And then we need to keep our promises to the Lord. And we need to lift others by sharing with them the blessings of the Atonement which have come in our lives.

We need to exemplify in our own lives the steady and prolonged faithfulness that the Lord expects of them. As we do, we will help them feel from the Spirit an assurance that if they will persist, they will hear the words from a loving Savior and Heavenly Father: "Well done, thou good and faithful servant: thou hast been faithful over a few things, I will make thee ruler over many things: enter thou into the joy of thy lord" (Matthew 25:21). And we who help them along the way will hear those words with joy.

We need to make plans which are not only wishes but covenants.

I testify that the Lord loves you and every child of God. I promise that as we follow inspired direction in this, the true Church of Jesus Christ, our youth and we who help and love them can be delivered safely to our home with Heavenly Father and the Savior to live in families and in joy forever.

FAMILIES UNDER COVENANT

I have a friend who returned to the Church after a period of inactivity largely because of the keys held by our prophet to seal families for eternity. This man and his wife love their two small children, a boy and a girl. Like other parents, he can foresee heavenly happiness when he reads these words: "And that same sociality which exists among us here will exist among us there, only it will be coupled with eternal glory, which glory we do not now enjoy" (Doctrine and Covenants 130:2).

That father knows the path to that glorious destination. It is not easy. He already knows that. It took faith in Jesus Christ, deep repentance, and a change in his heart that came with a kind bishop helping him feel the Lord's loving forgiveness.

Wonderful changes continued as he went to the holy temple for an endowment that the Lord described to those whom He empowered in the first temple in this dispensation. It was in Kirtland, Ohio. The Lord said of that:

"Wherefore, for this cause I gave unto you the commandment that ye should go to the Ohio; and there I will give unto you my law; and there you shall be endowed with power from on high;

"And from thence, . . . for I have a great work laid up in store, for Israel shall be saved, and I will lead them whithersoever I will, and no power shall stay my hand" (Doctrine and Covenants 38:32–33).

For my recently activated friend and for all the priesthood, a great work ahead is to lead in saving the part of Israel for which we are or will be responsible, our families. My friend and his wife knew that requires being sealed by the power of the Melchizedek Priesthood in a holy temple of God.

He asked that I perform the sealing. He and his wife wanted it done as soon as possible. But with the busy time of general conference approaching, I left it to the couple and their bishop to work with my secretary to find the best date.

Imagine my surprise and delight when the father told me in church that the sealing was set for April 3, the day in 1836 when Elijah, the translated prophet, was sent to the Kirtland Temple to give the sealing power to Joseph Smith and to Oliver Cowdery. Those keys reside in the Church today and will continue to the end of time (see Joseph Fielding Smith, "Sealing Power and Salvation," *Brigham Young University Speeches of the Year,* January 12, 1971, speeches.byu.edu).

It is the same divine authorization given by the Lord to Peter, as He had promised: "And I will give unto thee the keys of the kingdom of heaven: and whatsoever thou shalt bind on earth shall be bound in heaven: and whatsoever thou shalt loose on earth shall be loosed in heaven" (Matthew 16:19).

The return of Elijah blessed all who hold the priesthood. Elder Harold B. Lee made that clear as he spoke in general conference, quoting President Joseph Fielding Smith: "I hold the priesthood; you brethren here hold the priesthood; we have received the Melchizedek Priesthood—which was held by Elijah and by other prophets and by Peter, James and John. But while we have authority to baptize, while we have authority to lay on hands for the gift of the Holy Ghost and to ordain others and do all these things, without the sealing power we could do nothing, for there would be no validity to that which we did."

President Smith went on:

"The higher ordinances, the greater blessings which are essential to exaltation in the kingdom of God, and which can only be obtained in certain places, no man has a right to perform except as he receives the authority to do it from the one who holds the keys. . . .

The return of Elijah blessed all who hold the priesthood.

" . . . There is no man upon the face of this earth who has the right to go forth and administer in any of the ordinances of this gospel unless the President of the Church, who holds the keys, sanctions it. He has given us authority, he has put the sealing power in our priesthood, because he holds those keys" (quoted by Harold B. Lee, in Conference Report, October 1944, 75).

That same assurance came from President Boyd K. Packer as he wrote of the sealing power. Knowing these words are true is a comfort to me: "Peter was to hold the keys. Peter was to hold the sealing power, . . . to bind or seal on earth or to loose on earth and it would be so in the heavens. Those keys belong to the President of the Church—to the prophet, seer, and revelator. That sacred sealing power is with the Church now. Nothing is regarded with more sacred contemplation by those who know the significance of this authority. Nothing is more closely held. There are relatively few men who [hold] this sealing power upon the earth at any given time—in each temple are brethren who have been given the sealing power. No one can get it except from the prophet, seer, and revelator and President of The Church of Jesus Christ of Latter-day Saints" ("The Holy Temple," *Ensign,* October 2010, 34).

At the coming of Elijah, not only was power given to the priesthood, but also hearts were to be turned: "The spirit, power, and calling of Elijah is, that ye have power to hold the key of the revelation, ordinances, oracles, powers and endowments of the fullness of the Melchizedek Priesthood and of the kingdom of God on the earth; and to receive, obtain, and perform all the ordinances belonging to the kingdom of God, even unto the turning of the hearts of the fathers unto the children, and the hearts of the children unto the fathers, even those who are in heaven" (*Teachings of Presidents of the Church: Joseph Smith* [2007], 11).

> *There is nothing that has come or will come into your family as important as the sealing blessings. There is nothing more important than honoring the marriage and family covenants you have made or will make in the temples of God.*

That feeling of his heart turning has already come to my friend and to his family. It may have come to you in this meeting. As you read these words, you may have seen in your mind the face of your father or your mother. It may have been a sister or a brother. It may have been a daughter or a son.

They may be in the spirit world or continents away from you. But joy came from a feeling that connections with them are sure because you are or can be bound to them by priesthood ordinances that God will honor.

Melchizedek Priesthood holders who are fathers in sealed families have been taught what they must do. There is nothing that has come or will come into your family as important as the sealing blessings. There is nothing more important than honoring the marriage and family covenants you have made or will make in the temples of God.

The way to do that is clear. The Holy Spirit of Promise, through our obedience and sacrifice, must seal our temple covenants in order to be realized in the world to come. President Harold B. Lee explained what it means to be sealed by the Holy Spirit of Promise by quoting Elder Melvin J. Ballard: "We may deceive men but we cannot deceive the Holy Ghost, and our blessings will not be eternal unless they are also sealed by the Holy Spirit of promise. The Holy Ghost is one who reads the thoughts and hearts of men, and gives his sealing approval to the blessings pronounced upon their heads. Then it is binding, efficacious, and of full force" (quoted by Harold B. Lee, in Conference Report, October 1970, 111).

When Sister Eyring and I were sealed in the Logan Utah Temple, I did not understand then the full significance of that promise. I am still trying to understand all that it means, but my wife and I decided at the start of our nearly fifty years of marriage to invite the Holy Ghost as much as we could into our lives and into our family.

As a young father, sealed in the temple and with my heart turned to my wife and a young family, I met President Joseph Fielding Smith for the first time. In the First Presidency council room, where I had been invited, came an absolutely sure witness to me as President Harold B. Lee asked me, indicating President Smith, who was sitting next to him, "Do you believe that this man could be the prophet of God?"

President Smith had just entered the room and had not yet spoken a word. I am eternally grateful that I was able to answer because of what came down into my heart, "I know he is," and I knew it as surely as I knew the sun was shining that he held the priesthood sealing power for all the earth.

That experience gave his words great power for me and my wife when, in a conference session on April 6, 1972, President Joseph Fielding Smith gave the following counsel: "It is the will of the Lord to strengthen and preserve the family unit. We plead with fathers to take their rightful place as the head of the house. We ask mothers to sustain and support their husbands and to be lights to their children" ("Counsel to the Saints and to the World," *Ensign,* July 1972, 27).

Let me suggest four things you can do as a priesthood father to lift and lead your family home again to be with Heavenly Father and the Savior.

First, gain and keep a sure witness that the keys of the priesthood are with us and held by the President of the Church. Pray for that every day. The answer will come with an increase in determination to lead your family, in your feelings of hope, and with greater happiness in your service. You will be more cheerful and optimistic, a great blessing for your wife and family.

The second imperative is to love your wife. It will take faith and humility to put her interests above your own in the struggles of life. You have the responsibility to provide for and to nurture the family with her while serving others. That can at times consume all the energy and strength you have. Age and illness may increase your wife's needs. If you choose even then to put her happiness above your own, I promise you that your love for her will increase.

Third, enlist the entire family to love each other. President Ezra Taft Benson taught:

"In an eternal sense, salvation is a family affair. . . .

"Above all else, children need to know and feel they are loved, wanted, and appreciated. They need to be assured of that often. Obviously, this is a role parents should fill, and most often the mother can do it best" ("Salvation—a Family Affair," *Ensign,* July 1992, 2, 4).

But another crucial source for that feeling of being loved is love from other children in the family. Consistent care of brothers and sisters for each other will come only with persistent effort by parents and the help of God. You know that is true from experience in your own families. And it is confirmed each time you read of the family conflicts faced by righteous Lehi and his wife, Sariah, in the Book of Mormon record.

The successes they won provide a guide for us. They taught the gospel of Jesus Christ so well and so persistently that children and even some descendants over generations had hearts softened toward God and toward each other. For instance, Nephi and others wrote and reached out to family members who had been their enemies. The Spirit at times softened the hearts of thousands and replaced hatred with love.

One way for you to reproduce the successes of Father Lehi is by the way you lead family prayers and family time, such as family home evenings. Give children opportunities to pray, when they can pray, for each other in the circle who need blessings. Discern quickly the beginnings of discord and recognize acts of unselfish service, especially to each other. When they pray for each other and serve each other, hearts will be softened and turned to each other and to their parents.

The fourth opportunity to lead your family in the Lord's way comes when discipline is needed. We can meet our obligation to correct in the Lord's way and then lead our children toward eternal life.

You will remember the words, but you may not have seen their power for a Melchizedek Priesthood holder preparing his family for living in the same sociality that they will have in the celestial kingdom. You remember the words. They are so familiar:

"No power or influence can or ought to be maintained by virtue of the priesthood, only by persuasion, by long-suffering, by gentleness and meekness, and by love unfeigned;

"By kindness, and pure knowledge, which shall greatly enlarge the soul without hypocrisy, and without guile—

"Reproving betimes with sharpness, when moved upon by the Holy Ghost; and then showing forth afterwards an increase of love toward him whom thou hast reproved, lest he esteem thee to be his enemy;

Give children opportunities to pray, when they can pray, for each other in the circle who need blessings. Discern quickly the beginnings of discord and recognize acts of unselfish service, especially to each other.

"That he may know that thy faithfulness is stronger than the cords of death" (Doctrine and Covenants 121:41–44).

And later the promise comes of great worth for us as fathers in Zion: "The Holy Ghost shall be thy constant companion, and thy scepter an unchanging scepter of righteousness and truth; and thy dominion shall be an everlasting dominion, and without compulsory means it shall flow unto thee forever and ever" (Doctrine and Covenants 121:46).

That is a high standard for us, but when we with faith control our tempers and subdue our pride, the Holy Ghost gives His approval, and sacred promises and covenants become sure.

When we with faith control our tempers and subdue our pride, the Holy Ghost gives His approval, and sacred promises and covenants become sure.

You will succeed through your faith that the Lord sent back the keys of the priesthood, which are still with us—with a sure bond of love with your wife, with the Lord's help in turning the hearts of your children to each other and to their parents, and with love guiding you to correct and exhort in a way that invites the Spirit.

WALK IN THE LIGHT

For each of us, life is a journey. Heavenly Father designed it for us out of love. Each of us has unique experiences and characteristics, but our journey began in the same place before we were born into this world.

We all were taught by Elohim, the Father of our spirits. We loved Him and wanted to be like Him and to be with Him forever. He told us plainly what it would require for us to have that joy. We would have to receive a physical body, with all of the trials that would bring. We would be subject to illness and have within our bodies the processes which would finally lead to death. And our bodies would have in them powerful cravings for physical satisfaction.

Heavenly Father explained to us what it would take to make the journey from where we were then to be with Him forever and live the life that He lives. We would make the journey through life without a memory of our time with Him in the spirit world. And the only way back to Him would be for us to overcome physical death and the effects of sin which would come from our breaking commandments. He told us that we could not overcome the effects of either death or sin by ourselves—without our having a Savior who would break the bands of death and provide a way for us to be washed clean from the sin which we would surely commit.

You know from the scriptures revealed by God through prophets that there was a rebellion in the spirit world when the plan for our journey was offered to us. Those who rebelled did not want to accept and to depend upon a Savior nor run any risk that they might not return again to Heavenly Father. You were among the brave, the faithful, and the true in that conflict. You accepted the Savior and the plan for this journey to return to the joy of our Heavenly Father's presence.

You are remarkable, even among those who chose right in the contest in the spirit world. You qualified to come into mortality and to make this journey at a time when the gospel of Jesus Christ was on the earth. And among the billions of Heavenly Father's children now living, you were privileged to find the gospel of Jesus Christ and His true Church. You have chosen to make the journey of life walking in the light.

Every child of Heavenly Father born in the world is given at birth, as a free gift, the Light of Christ. You have felt that. It is the sense of what is right and what is wrong and what is true and what is false. That has been with you since your journey in life began. The fact that you were baptized and received the Holy Ghost is evidence that you chose to walk in the Light of Christ.

When you were confirmed a member of the Church, you were given the right to have the Holy Ghost as your companion. The Holy Ghost is a powerful source of light to recognize truth, to follow and love the Lord Jesus Christ, and to find your way back to God after this life.

But the spirit who led the rebellion in the world before still opposes the plan and wants you to be miserable. He wants you never to find your way home again. That enemy of your soul knows you and your goodness. He knows that if he can turn you away from walking in the light, he can both capture you and stop you from helping others along the journey. He knows how good you are and your power to teach and influence hundreds of Heavenly Father's children in this life—and thousands over the generations that will follow your path. If he can get you to wander away from the light on your journey, he can do harm and bring misery to many.

God recognizes your great importance and that you have chosen to walk in the light He offers you. Such choices are not always easy to see clearly. You make choices every day and almost every hour that keep you walking in the light or moving away toward darkness. Some of the most important choices are about what you set your heart upon.

The spirit who led the rebellion in the world before still opposes the plan and wants you to be miserable. He wants you never to find your way home again. That enemy of your soul knows you and your goodness. He knows that if he can turn you away from walking in the light, he can both capture you and stop you from helping others along the journey.

There are so many things you may consider desirable. For instance, all of us want, to some degree, the approval of other people. All of us feel a need for friends. All of us are searching for some evidence that we are persons of worth. We make choices based on those desires. Some might lead us away from the light God offers us as a guide. Some may brighten that light by which we can find our way.

As I look back, I realize that I was unaware of the importance of some of those desires and choices. I wanted to be selected for athletic teams. I wanted to do well in school. I wanted to find good and true friends. And when I made the choices that came from those desires, more than I realized, I was either moving away from the light or toward it.

Some of my achievements and some of my friends were major factors in my sensing light. Others, more than I knew at the time, were edging me away from the light. In important and long-lasting ways, choices I made to satisfy my desires for companionship and a sense of recognition were taking me either toward or away from the light to guide my path.

Long ago Heavenly Father, through His prophets, gave us a way to know which choices matter most and why—and how to make them. The best summary I know is in the words from Moroni as he quotes his father, Mormon:

"But behold, that which is of God inviteth and enticeth to do good continually; wherefore, every thing which inviteth and enticeth to do good, and to love God, and to serve him, is inspired of God.

"Wherefore, take heed . . . that ye do not judge that which is evil to be of God, or that which is good and of God to be of the devil.

"For behold, my brethren, it is given unto you to judge, that ye may know good from evil; and the way to judge is as plain, that ye may know with a perfect knowledge, as the daylight is from the dark night" (Moroni 7:13–15).

The scriptures tell us the source and the power of the light.

"For behold, the Spirit of Christ is given to every man, that he may know good from evil; wherefore, I show unto you the way to judge; for every thing which inviteth to do good, and to persuade to believe in Christ, is sent forth by the power and gift of Christ; wherefore ye may know with a perfect knowledge it is of God.

"But whatsoever thing persuadeth men to do evil, and believe not in Christ, and deny him, and serve not God, then ye may know with a perfect knowledge it is of the devil; for after this manner doth the devil work, for he persuadeth no man to do good, no, not one; neither do his angels; neither do they who subject themselves unto him" (Moroni 7:16–17).

I can see now, better than I could as a young man, how I might have used that guidance. There were sports teams that had players and coaches who influenced me to do good. There were some that did not. There were friends, some of them not members of the Church of Jesus Christ, who by their example influenced me to do good and to remember the Savior.

There were schoolmates and teachers whose approval and friendship I sought who somehow made me want to do good and enhance my feelings for the Savior. I was blessed to find my way. But I would have done even better had I understood both the importance of my choices and the way to choose.

Mormon knew that. Had I read more carefully his words in the Book of Mormon, and others like them, I would have been even more blessed and more protected. Here are Mormon's words:

"Seeing that ye know the light by which ye may judge, which light is the light of Christ, see that ye do not judge wrongfully; for with that same judgment which ye judge ye shall also be judged.

"Wherefore, . . . ye should search diligently in the light of Christ that ye may know good from evil; and if ye will lay hold upon every good thing, and condemn it not, ye certainly will be a child of Christ.

"And now, . . . how is it possible that ye can lay hold upon every good thing?" (Moroni 7:18–20).

It is by faith that you can lay hold upon every good thing. Just as you are marked as a target by the enemy of righteousness, you have

WALK IN THE LIGHT

been protected and watched over by your Heavenly Father and the Lord Jesus Christ. They know you. They know all of the forces and individuals around you. They know what is ahead of you. And so They know which of the choices you make, which of the desires you decide to satisfy, and which of the circumstances around you will make the most difference in keeping you walking in the light. I testify that by the Spirit of Christ and by the Holy Ghost, you may walk confidently in whatever difficulties will come. Because you are so valuable, some of your trials may be severe. You need never be discouraged or afraid. The way through difficulties has always been prepared for you, and you will find it if you exercise faith.

Because you are so valuable, some of your trials may be severe. You need never be discouraged or afraid. The way through difficulties has always been prepared for you, and you will find it if you exercise faith.

You must have faith to pray. You must have faith to ponder the word of God. You must have faith to do those things and go to those places which invite the Spirit of Christ and the Holy Ghost.

When you walk in the light, you will feel some of the warmth and the happiness that will finally be yours when you are welcomed home again with the hundreds and perhaps thousands of others whom you will bring with you, who have walked in the light because you did.

SPIRITUAL PREPAREDNESS: START EARLY AND BE STEADY

Most of us have thought about how to prepare for storms. We have seen and felt the suffering of women, men, and children, and of the aged and the weak, caught in hurricanes, tsunamis, wars, and droughts. One reaction is to ask, "How can I be prepared?" And there is a rush to buy and put away whatever people think they might need for the day they might face such calamities.

But there is another even more important preparation we must make for tests that are certain to come to each of us. That preparation must be started far in advance because it takes time. What we will need then can't be bought. It can't be borrowed. It doesn't store well. And it has to have been used regularly and recently.

What we will need in our day of testing is a spiritual preparation. It is to have developed faith in Jesus Christ so powerful that we can pass the test of life upon which everything for us in eternity depends. That test is part of the purpose God had for us in the Creation.

The Prophet Joseph Smith gave us the Lord's description of the test we face. Our Heavenly Father created the world with His Son, Jesus Christ. We have these words to tell us about the purpose of the Creation: "We will go down, for there is space there, and we will take of these materials, and we will make an earth whereon these may dwell; And we will prove them herewith, to see if they will do all things whatsoever the Lord their God shall command them" (Abraham 3:24–25).

So, the great test of life is to see whether we will hearken to and obey God's commands in the midst of the storms of life. It is not to endure storms, but to choose the right while they rage. And the tragedy of life is to fail in that test and so fail to qualify to return in glory to our heavenly home.

The great test of life is to see whether we will hearken to and obey God's commands in the midst of the storms of life. It is not to endure storms, but to choose the right while they rage.

We are the spirit children of a Heavenly Father. He loved us and He taught us before we were born into this world. He told us that He wished to give us all that He had. To qualify for that gift we had to receive mortal bodies and be tested. Because of those mortal bodies, we would face pain, sickness, and death.

We would be subject to temptations through the desires and weaknesses that came with our mortal bodies. Subtle and powerful forces of evil would tempt us to surrender to those temptations. Life would have storms in which we would have to make choices using faith in things we could not see with our natural eyes.

We were promised that we would have Jehovah, Jesus Christ, as our Savior and Redeemer. He would assure that we would all be resurrected. And He would make it possible for us to pass the test of life if we exercised faith in Him by being obedient. We shouted for joy at the good news.

A passage from the Book of Mormon, another witness of Jesus

Christ, describes how hard the test is and what it will take to pass it:

"Therefore, cheer up your hearts, and remember that ye are free to act for yourselves—to choose the way of everlasting death or the way of eternal life.

"Wherefore, my beloved brethren, reconcile yourselves to the will of God, and not to the will of the devil and the flesh; and remember, after ye are reconciled unto God, that it is only in and through the grace of God that ye are saved.

"Wherefore, may God raise you from death by the power of the resurrection, and also from everlasting death by the power of the atonement, that ye may be received into the eternal kingdom of God, that ye may praise him through grace divine. Amen" (2 Nephi 10:23–25).

It will take unshakable faith in the Lord Jesus Christ to choose the way to eternal life. It is by using that faith we can know the will of God. It is by acting on that faith we build the strength to do the will of God. And it is by exercising that faith in Jesus Christ that we can resist temptation and gain forgiveness through the Atonement.

We will need to have developed and nurtured faith in Jesus Christ long before Satan hits us, as he will, with doubts and appeals to our carnal desires and with lying voices saying that good is bad and that there is no sin. Those spiritual storms are already raging. We can expect that they will worsen until the Savior returns.

However much faith to obey God we now have, we will need to strengthen it continually and keep it refreshed constantly. We can do that by deciding now to be more quick to obey and more determined to endure. Learning to start early and to be steady are the keys to spiritual preparation. Procrastination and inconsistency are its mortal enemies.

Let me suggest to you four settings in which to practice quick and steady obedience. One is the command to feast upon the word of God. A second is to pray always. A third is the commandment to be a full-tithe payer. And the fourth is to escape from sin and its terrible effects. Each takes faith to start and then to persevere. And all can strengthen your capacity to know and obey the Lord's commands.

You may remember, from some years ago, President Gordon B. Hinckley's invitation to all the Saints to read the Book of Mormon through by the end of the year. He said: "Without reservation I promise you that if each of you will observe this simple program, regardless of how many times you previously may have read the Book of Mormon, there will come into your lives and into your homes an added measure of the Spirit of the Lord, a strengthened resolution to walk in obedience to

> *However much faith to obey God we now have, we will need to strengthen it continually and keep it refreshed constantly. We can do that by deciding now to be more quick to obey and more determined to endure.*

His commandments, and a stronger testimony of the living reality of the Son of God" ("A Testimony Vibrant and True," *Ensign*, August 2005, 6).

That was the very promise of increased faith we would need to be spiritually prepared. But if we delayed the start of our obedience to that inspired invitation, the number of pages we had to read each day grew larger. If we then missed reading for even a few days, the chance of failure grew. That's why I chose to read ahead of my daily plan to be sure I would qualify for the promised blessings of the spirit of resolution and testimony of Jesus Christ. I have learned about starting at the moment a command from God comes and being steady in obedience.

More than that, as I read in the Book of Mormon, I prayed that the Holy Ghost would help me know what God would have me do. There is a promise of that plea being answered in the book itself: "Wherefore, I said unto you, feast upon the words of Christ; for behold, the words of Christ will tell you all things what ye should do" (2 Nephi 32:3).

I determined that I would act quickly on what the Holy Ghost told me I should do as I read and pondered the Book of Mormon. When I completed the project in December, I had had many experiences of stretching my faith to be obedient. And so my faith was strengthened. And I knew from my own experience what comes from going to the scriptures early and consistently to know what God wants me to do and then doing it. If we do that, we will be better prepared for the greater storms when they come.

Those of us who accepted the prophet's counsel and finished the Book of Mormon that year then had a choice of what to do after January 1. We could have chosen to sigh with relief and to say to ourselves: "I have built a great reservoir of faith by starting early and being steady in obedience. I will store it away against the times when I will be tested in storms." There is a better way to prepare, because great faith has a short shelf life. We can decide to persist in studying the words of Christ in the scriptures and the teachings of living prophets. This is what I have chosen to do. I go back to the Book of Mormon and drink deeply and often. And I am grateful for what the prophet's challenge and promise did to teach me how to gain greater faith and maintain it.

Personal prayer can also build our faith to do what God commands. We are commanded to pray *always* that we will not be overcome. Some of the protection we need will be direct intervention of God. But more of it will come from building our faith to obey. We can pray every day to know what God would have us do. We can commit to start to do it quickly when the answer comes. My experience is that He always answers such

Great faith has a short shelf life.

petitions. Then, we can choose to obey. As we do, we will build faith enough that we will not be overcome. And we will gain the faith to go back again and again for further instruction. When the storms come, we will be ready to go and do what the Lord commands.

The Savior showed us a great example of such a prayer of submission. He prayed in the Garden of Gethsemane as He worked out the Atonement that His Father's will would be done. He knew that His Father's will would be for Him to do what was so painful and so terrible that we cannot comprehend it. He prayed not simply to accept the Father's will but to do it. He showed us the way to pray in perfect and determined submission.

The principle of exercising faith early and steadily applies as well to the commandment to pay tithing. We should not wait until the annual tithing settlement to decide to be a full-tithe payer. We can decide now. It takes time to learn to control our spending with faith that what we have comes from God. It takes faith to pay our tithing promptly and without procrastination.

If we decide now to be a full-tithe payer and if we are steady in paying it, blessings will flow throughout the year, as well as at the time of tithing settlement. By our decision now to be a full-tithe payer and our steady efforts to obey, we will be strengthened in our faith and, in time, our hearts will be softened. It is that change in our hearts through the Atonement of Jesus Christ, beyond the offering of our money or goods, that makes it possible for the Lord to promise full-tithe payers protection in the last days (see Doctrine and Covenants 64:23). We can have confidence that we will qualify for that blessing of protection if we commit now to pay a full tithe and are steady in doing it.

The same power of an early choice to exercise faith and to be persistent in obedience applies to gaining the faith to resist temptation and to gain forgiveness. The best time to resist temptation is early. The best time to repent is now. The enemy of our souls will place thoughts in our minds to tempt us. We can decide early to exercise faith, to cast out evil thoughts before we act on them. And we can choose quickly to repent when we do sin, before Satan can weaken our faith and bind us. Seeking forgiveness is always better now than later.

We can decide early to exercise faith, to cast out evil thoughts before we act on them. And we can choose quickly to repent when we do sin, before Satan can weaken our faith and bind us. Seeking forgiveness is always better now than later.

As my father lay in his bed near death, I asked him if he didn't think it was a time to repent and pray for forgiveness for any sins that were not yet resolved with God. He probably heard a little hint in my voice that he might fear death and the Judgment. He just chuckled quietly, smiled up at me, and said, "Oh no, Hal, I've been repenting as I went along."

Decisions now to exercise faith and be steady in obedience will in time produce great faith and assurance. That is the spiritual preparedness we all will need. And it will qualify us in the moments of crisis to receive the Lord's promise that "if ye are prepared ye shall not fear" (Doctrine and Covenants 38:30).

That will be true when we face the storms of life and the prospect of death. A loving Heavenly Father and His Beloved Son have given us all the help They can to pass the test of life set before us. But we must decide to obey and then do it. We build the faith to pass the tests of obedience over time and through our daily choices. We can decide now to do quickly whatever God asks of us. And we can decide to be steady in the small tests of obedience which build the faith to carry us through the great tests, which will surely come.

I know that through the Holy Ghost we can learn what God would have us do. I testify that He can give us the power to do what He asks of us, whatever it is and whatever trials may come. I pray that we will choose to obey the Lord quickly, always, in quiet times and in storms. As we do, our faith will be strengthened, we will find peace in this life, and we will gain the assurance that we and our families can qualify for eternal life in the world to come.

PERSONAL GROWTH
THROUGH
HELPING OTHERS

OUR PERFECT EXAMPLE

Different as we are in circumstances and experiences, we share a desire to become better than we are. There may be a few who mistakenly feel they are good enough and a few who have given up trying to be better. But, for all, the message of the restored gospel of Jesus Christ is that we can and must expect to become better as long as we live.

Part of that expectation is set for us in a revelation given by God to the Prophet Joseph Smith. It describes the day when we will meet the Savior, as we all will. It tells us what to do to prepare and what to expect.

It is in the book of Moroni: "Wherefore, my beloved brethren, pray unto the Father with all the energy of heart, that ye may be filled with this love, which he hath bestowed upon all who are true followers of his Son, Jesus Christ; that ye may become the sons of God; that when he shall appear we shall be like him, for we shall see him as he is; that we may have this hope; that we may be purified even as he is pure. Amen" (Moroni 7:48).

That ought to help you understand why any believing Latter-day Saint is an optimist about what lies ahead for him or her, however difficult the present may be. We believe that through living the gospel of Jesus Christ we can become like the Savior, who is perfect. Considering the attributes of Jesus Christ should quash the pride of the self-satisfied person who thinks he or she has no need to improve. And even the most humble person can take hope in the invitation to become like the Savior.

How that wonderful transformation will happen is captured for me in a song written for children. I remember watching the faces of a room full of children singing it on a Sunday. Each of the children was leaning forward, almost to the front of the chair. I could see light in their eyes and determination in their faces as they sang with gusto:

> *I'm trying to be like Jesus; I'm following in his ways.*
> *I'm trying to love as he did, in all that I do and say.*
> *At times I am tempted to make a wrong choice,*
> *But I try to listen as the still small voice whispers,*
> *"Love one another as Jesus loves you.*
> *Try to show kindness in all that you do.*
> *Be gentle and loving in deed and in thought,*
> *For these are the things Jesus taught."*
> (Janice Kapp Perry, "I'm Trying to Be like Jesus,"
> *Children's Songbook* [1989], 78–79)

It seemed to me that they were not just singing; they were declaring their determination. Jesus Christ was their example. To be like Him was their fixed goal. And their eager looks and their shining eyes convinced me that they had no doubts. They expected to succeed. They believed that the instruction of the Savior to be perfect was not a hope but a command. And they were sure He had prepared the way.

That determination and confidence can and must be in the heart of every Latter-day Saint. The Savior has prepared the way through His Atonement and His example. And even the children who sang that song knew how.

Love is the motivating principle by which the Lord leads us along the way toward becoming like Him, *our perfect example.* Our way of life, hour by hour, must be filled with the love of God and love for others. There is no surprise in that, since the Lord proclaimed those as the first and great commandments. It is love of God that will lead us to keep His commandments. And love of others is at the heart of our capacity to obey Him.

Just as Jesus used a child in His mortal ministry as an example for the people of the pure love they must and could have to be like Him, He has offered us the family as an example of an ideal setting in which we can learn how to love as He loves.

Considering the attributes of Jesus Christ should quash the pride of the self-satisfied person who thinks he or she has no need to improve. And even the most humble person can take hope in the invitation to become like the Savior.

That is because the greatest joys and the greatest sorrows we experience are in family relationships. The joys come from putting the welfare of others above our own. That is what love is. And the sorrow comes primarily from selfishness, which is the absence of love. The ideal God holds for us is to form families in the way most likely to lead to happiness and away from sorrow. A man and a woman are to make sacred covenants that they will put the welfare and happiness of the other at the center of their lives. Children are to be born into a family where the parents hold the needs of children equal to their own in importance. And children are to love parents and each other.

That is the ideal of a loving family. In many of our homes, there are the words "Our Family Can Be Together Forever." There is a gravestone near my home of a mother and grandmother. She and her husband were sealed in the temple of God to each other and to their posterity for time and all eternity. The inscription on the gravestone reads, "Please, no empty chairs." She asked for that inscription because she knew that whether the family will be together depends on the choices each family member makes. The word "please" is there because neither God nor she can compel another to choose happiness. And there is Satan, who wants misery, not happiness, in families in this life and in the next.

It is love of God that will lead us to keep His commandments. And love of others is at the heart of our capacity to obey Him.

My hope is to suggest some choices which may seem difficult but that would assure you that you have qualified for there to be no empty chairs in your family in the world to come.

First, I give counsel to husbands and wives. Pray for the love which allows you to see the good in your companion. Pray for the love that makes weaknesses and mistakes seem small. Pray for the love to make your companion's joy your own. Pray for the love to want to lessen the load and soften the sorrows of your companion.

I saw this in my parents' marriage. In my mother's final illness, the more uncomfortable she became, the more giving her comfort became the dominant intent of my father's life. He asked that the hospital set up a bed in her room. He was determined to be there to be sure that she wanted for nothing. He walked the miles to work each morning and back to her side at night through those difficult times for her. I believe it was a gift from God to him that his power to love grew when it mattered so much to her. I think he was doing what Jesus would have done out of love.

Now I give counsel to the parents of a wandering child. The Savior is the perfect example of persisting in love. You remember His words of comfort to the people among the Nephites who had rejected His earlier invitation to come to Him. He spoke to the survivors of the destruction which came after His Crucifixion: "O ye house of Israel whom I have spared, how oft will I gather you as a hen gathereth her chickens under her wings, if ye will repent and return unto me with full purpose of heart" (3 Nephi 10:6).

The story of the prodigal son gives us all hope. The prodigal remembered home, as will your children. They will feel your love drawing them back to you. Elder

Pray for the love that makes weaknesses and mistakes seem small.

Orson F. Whitney, in a general conference of 1929, gave a remarkable promise, which I know is true, to the faithful parents who honor the temple sealing to their children: "Though some of the sheep may wander, the eye of the Shepherd is upon them, and sooner or later they will feel the tentacles of Divine Providence reaching out after them and drawing them back to the fold."

Then he goes on to say: "Pray for your careless and disobedient children; hold on to them with your faith. Hope on, trust on, till you see the salvation of God" (in Conference Report, April 1929, 110). You can pray for your children, love them, and reach out to them with confidence that Jesus reaches for them with you. When you keep trying, you are doing what Jesus does.

Now, here is my counsel to children. The Lord gave you a commandment with a promise: "Honor thy father and thy mother, that thy days may be long upon the land which the Lord thy God giveth thee" (Mosiah 13:20). It is the only one of the Ten Commandments with a promise. You may not have parents that are living. In some cases, you may not feel that your parents are worthy of the honor and respect of their children. You may not even have ever known them. But you owe them life. And in every case, even if your life is not lengthened, its quality will be improved simply by remembering your parents with honor.

Now to those who have adopted other people's families as if they were their own: I have friends who remember my children's birthdays better than I do. My wife and I have had friends who seldom failed to visit or to remember a holiday with us. I often am touched when someone begins a conversation, "How is your family?" and then waits to hear the answer with love showing in their face. They seem attentive when I go through a description of the life of each of my children. Their love helps me to feel more keenly the love of the Savior for our children. In their question, I can sense that they are feeling what Jesus feels and asking what He would ask.

For all of us it may be hard to see in our lives an increasing power to love and to see ourselves becoming more like the Savior, *our perfect example*. I wish to encourage you. You have had evidences that you are moving along the road to becoming more like Jesus. It will help to remember how you have felt, at times, like a little child, even in the midst of cares and trials. Think of those children singing the song. Think of the times you felt, perhaps recently, as those little children did singing, "I'm trying to be like Jesus; I'm following in his ways." You will remember that Jesus asked His disciples to bring the children to Him and said, "Suffer

50

the little children to come unto me, . . . for of such is the kingdom of God" (Mark 10:14). You have felt the peace of a pure little child at times when you have tried to be like Jesus.

It may have come when you were baptized. He did not need baptism, because He was pure. But when you were baptized, you had the feeling of being washed clean, like a little child. When He was baptized, the heavens were opened, and He heard the voice of His Heavenly Father: "This is my beloved Son, in whom I am well pleased" (Matthew 3:17). You heard no voice, but you felt the approval of Heavenly Father for having done what Jesus did.

You have felt it in your family when you asked the pardon of your spouse or forgave a child for some mistake or disobedience. These moments will come more often as you try to do the things you know Jesus would do. Because of His

You have had evidences that you are moving along the road to becoming more like Jesus. It will help to remember how you have felt, at times, like a little child, even in the midst of cares and trials. You have felt the peace of a pure little child at times when you have tried to be like Jesus.

Atonement for you, your childlike obedience will bring a feeling of love of the Savior for you and your love for Him. That is one of the gifts that is promised to His faithful disciples. And this gift can come not only to you alone but also to the loving members of your family. The promise was given in 3 Nephi: "And all thy children shall be taught of the Lord; and great shall be the peace of thy children" (3 Nephi 22:13).

I hope you will go out today looking for opportunities to do as He did and to love as He loves. I can promise you the peace that you felt as a child will come to you often and it will linger with you. The promise is true that He made to His disciples: "Peace I leave with you, my peace I give unto you: not as the world giveth, give I unto you" (John 14:27).

None of us is perfect yet. But we can have frequent assurance that we are following along the way. He leads us, and He beckons for us to follow Him.

A Child of God

General James Gavin was a young general in the American army during World War II. He commanded the 82nd Airborne Division. He led them in the invasion of Sicily. There were casualties there. He parachuted with them behind enemy lines during the invasions in France. They lost more men there. Then he led them in the bloody battles in Belgium when the Germans counterattacked, taking a terrible toll among his troops.

General Gavin's soldiers were given some well-earned leave. Some of them went to Paris. A general from another Allied army saw them there. Later, when he met General Gavin, he said that he had never seen better-looking soldiers. General Gavin's laconic reply was that they ought to look good: they were the survivors.

You are among the survivors. By making the right choices, and with the help of uncounted servants of God, you have made it through a hail of spiritual bullets. There have been tens of thousands of casualties. You know some of them because they are your friends, your spirit brothers and your sisters. You are more than simply the survivors of that spiritual war. You are the future of the Church. God knows that. And so He now asks more of you than He has asked of those who were here before you, because the kingdom will need more. And Satan knows that you are the future of the Church, which gives me a solemn obligation to warn you of the hazards ahead and to describe how to survive them as you rise to the privileges God will give you.

You are under mandate to pursue excellence. You, along with every Latter-day Saint, need to continue learning throughout your whole life. And yet the Lord gives the warning of danger as He gives the charge. You remember the words from the Book of Mormon:

"O that cunning plan of the evil one! O the vainness, and the frailties, and the foolishness of men! When they are learned they think they are wise, and they hearken not unto the counsel of God, for they set it aside, supposing they know of themselves, wherefore, their wisdom is foolishness and it profiteth them not. And they shall perish" (2 Nephi 9:28).

You are to pursue excellence while avoiding pride, the great spiritual destroyer. Most people would question whether it is possible to pursue excellence in anything without feeling some measure of pride.

A professional basketball player in the National Basketball Association sat next to me on a plane just after President Ezra Taft Benson gave a talk warning about pride. In general conference President Benson had said that there was no such thing as righteous pride. My seatmate hadn't heard the talk, so I told him about it and asked whether he could excel in the NBA down under the basket if he were stripped of all pride. His quiet answer was that he doubted that he could survive at all, let alone excel.

A Broadway star had a colorful way of expressing his opinion about the place of pride in his work. He had been hired to be the lead in a production of *Fiddler on the Roof* with a cast of college students. I was asked to give a prayer with the cast on opening night. The Broadway veteran, who had played the part hundreds of times, stood at the back of a ring of students gathered around me just before the curtain was to go up. He looked puzzled.

As I recall now, I pleaded with God that the members of the cast would be lifted above their natural abilities, that the stage equipment would function well, that the hearts of the audience would be softened, and that they would be touched. I can't remember much else of the prayer, but I can remember what happened just after I said "Amen."

The Broadway star jumped into the air, landed on the stage with the sound of an explosion coming from his heavy boots, slapped his hands to his sides, and then thrust them into the air and shouted, "Okay, now let's go for it!" If the audience heard his bellow, and I can't imagine that they didn't, they must have expected the cast to come charging through the curtain out into the audience bent on some kind of mayhem.

You are to pursue excellence while avoiding pride, the great spiritual destroyer. Most people would question whether it is possible to pursue excellence in anything without feeling some measure of pride.

I can only assume that he was determined to counteract the terrible mistake he had just witnessed. The last thing on earth he wanted was to go on a stage with a bunch of amateur actors who had been infected with humility.

I will not attempt to tell you how to pursue excellence and humility simultaneously in the NBA or on Broadway. In those settings, if you get there, you will have to find your own way.

But I will tell you that not only can you pursue excellence and humility at the same time to avoid spiritual danger but that the way to humility is also the doorway to excellence. The best antidote I know for pride also can produce in us the characteristics that lead to excellence.

Let's start with the problem of pride. There is more than one antidote for it. Some of them don't take any action on our part. Life delivers them. Failure, illness, disaster, and losses of all kinds have a way of chipping away at pride. But they come in uneven doses. Too much can come at one time and crush us with discouragement or embitter us. Or the antidote can come too late, after pride has made us vulnerable to temptation.

There is something we can choose to do in our daily life that will provide a constant protection against pride. It is simply to remember who God is and what it means to be His child.

There is a better way. There is something we can choose to do in our daily life that will provide a constant protection against pride. It is simply to remember who God is and what it means to be His child. That is what we covenant to do each time we take the sacrament, promising always to remember the Savior. Because of what has been revealed to us about the plan of salvation, remembering Him can produce the humility that will be our protection. And then, as we will see later, that same choice to remember Him will in time produce in us greater power to learn both what we need to know for living in this world and in the life to come.

Remembering the Savior produces humility this way: Because we are blessed by revelation from prophets in this dispensation, we see His part in the plan of salvation, and from that we come to know both our loving Heavenly Father and what it means to be His spirit child.

When we remember the Savior we see Him as the creator of all things, about which the wisest of us knows so little. We remember our dependence on His sacrifice when we think of the fall of man and of our own sins. We remember His unfailing love for us and His arms extended in invitation to us when we think of the little we understand of what He did to atone for our sins. We remember that we will only come again to our Heavenly Father to live forever in families by obeying His commandments and having the Holy Ghost to guide us. And we remember His example of complete submission to the will of His Father and our Father.

Those memories, if we choose to invite them, can produce a powerful blend of courage and meekness. No problem is too hard for us with His help. No price is too great to pay for what He offers us. And still in our greatest successes we feel as little children. And in our greatest sacrifices we still feel in His debt, wanting to give more. That is a humility which is energizing, not enervating. We can choose that shield as a protection against pride. And when we make that choice, to remember Him, we are at the same time choosing to do what can lead us to acquire the characteristics of great learners.

In our greatest sacrifices we still feel in His debt, wanting to give more. That is a humility which is energizing, not enervating.

That view of what it means to be a child of God, if we choose to act on it as reality, will lead us to do what great learners do. Those habits are not unique to those who understand and have faith in the revelations of God. The principles of learning work the same for all people, whether or not they know and believe in the plan of salvation. But we have an advantage. We can remember the Savior, think again of what the revelations tell us about who we are, and then we can choose to act on that reality. That will make us better learners.

I'll mention just a few of those habits of great learners. In each instance you will recognize them. You have known great scholars and observed them carefully. There are some common patterns in what they do. And each of those habits will be strengthened by acting in our daily life on our faith that the plan of salvation is a description of reality.

The first characteristic behavior is to welcome correction. You may have seen that in students, for instance, who value wise editing of their writing. If they seek that correction, study it when they get it, and then revise what they have written, they become better writers. In the same way, the scientists who submit their work to be reviewed by those who understand their methods and their research findings make the most rapid progress. And the wise student of a new language seeks not the tutor who praises whatever they say but one who won't let a mispronounced word or an error in conjugating a verb pass uncorrected.

That desire for correction, a mark of great learners, comes naturally to a Latter-day Saint who knows and values what it means to be a child of God. For him or her it begins with seeking frequent correction directly from our Heavenly Father. One of the most valuable forms of personal revelation can come before private prayer. It can come in the quiet contemplation of how we might have offended, disappointed, or displeased our Heavenly Father. The Spirit of Christ and the Holy Ghost will help us feel rebuke and at the same time the encouragement to repent. Then prayers asking for forgiveness become less general and the chance to have the Atonement work in our life becomes greater.

We have another advantage as Latter-day Saints. We know that a loving Father has allowed us to live in a time when Jesus Christ has called prophets and others to serve as judges in Israel. Because of that we listen to a prophet's voice or sit in counsel with a bishop with the hope that we will hear correction.

That is true because we know something of the nature of God and our own condition. There was a fall. There was a veil placed over our memories. We walk by faith. Because of our mortality, we all sin. We cannot return to our Father unless we repent and, by keeping covenants, are washed clean through the sacrifice of His Son. We know He has

We see the giving and the taking of correction as priceless and sacred.

placed servants to offer us both His covenants and His correction. We see the giving and the taking of correction as priceless and sacred. That is at least one of the reasons why the Lord warned us to seek as our teachers only men and women who are inspired of Him. And that is one of the reasons why we welcome prophets to lead us.

A second characteristic of great learners is that they keep commitments. Any community functions better when people in it keep their promises to live up to its accepted standards. But for a learner and for a community of learners, that keeping of commitments has special significance.

That is why we sometimes describe formal fields of study as "disciplines." Different fields have different rules. In physics there are some rules about how to decide to believe something is true. That is sometimes called the "scientific method." But when we move over into engineering or geology, there are some slightly different rules. In history or French literature or accounting, we will find even more diverse sets of rules. You will someday, if you haven't yet, experience the turmoil of trying to learn in a discipline that is trying to agree on new rules but failing.

What all disciplines have in common is a search for rules and a commitment to them. And what all great learners have is a deep appreciation for finding better rules and a commitment to keeping them. That is why great learners are careful about what commitments they make and then keeping them.

The Latter-day Saints who see themselves in all they do as children of God take naturally to making and keeping commitments. The plan of salvation is marked by covenants. We promise to obey commandments. In return, God promises blessings in this life and for eternity. He is exact in what He requires, and He is perfect in keeping His word. Because He loves us and because the purpose of the plan is to become like Him, He requires exactness of us. And the promises He makes to us always include the power to grow in our capacity to keep covenants. He makes it possible for us to know His rules. When we try with all our hearts to meet His standards, He gives us the companionship of the Holy Ghost. That in turn increases our power both to keep commitments and to discern what is good and true. And that is the power to learn, both in our temporal studies and in the learning we need for eternity.

There is a third characteristic you have seen in great learners. They work hard. When people quit working, they quit learning, which is one of the hazards of getting too much recognition early in a career and taking it too seriously.

You will notice that the learners who can sustain that power to work hard over a lifetime generally don't do it for grades or to make tenure in a university or for prizes in the world. Something else drives them. For some it may be an innate curiosity to see how things work.

For the child of God who has enough faith in the plan of salvation to treat it as reality, hard work is the only reasonable option. Life at its longest is short. What we do here determines the rest of our condition for eternity. God our Father has offered us everything He has and asks only that we give Him all we have to give. That is an exchange so imbalanced in our favor that no effort would be too much and no hours too long in service to Him, to the Savior, and to our Father's children. Hard work is the natural result of simply knowing and believing what it means to be a child of God.

For the child of God who has enough faith in the plan of salvation to treat it as reality, hard work is the only reasonable option. Life at its longest is short. What we do here determines the rest of our condition for eternity.

That leads to the description of another characteristic of a great learner: great learners help other people. Every great learner I have ever met has helped me, or tried to help me, or clearly wished to help me. That could seem to you a paradox, since people trying hard to learn might justifiably be absorbed only in themselves and what they are trying to learn. Now I know the rebuke you might give me. I'll anticipate your correction. You would say, "Is that true of all great learners?"

I answer, "Of course not." There are renowned scholars who are selfish and even unkind to those they consider less gifted. You will meet them if you haven't yet. But those who learn most over long lives seem to have a generous view of others, both in what they can learn from other people and the capacity others have to learn. Those who can't suffer fools gladly become more foolish themselves. They have shut themselves off from what they can learn from others.

Those who learn best seem to see that everyone they meet knows something they don't and may have a capacity they don't have. Because of that you will find that the best learners make the best company.

That kindly and optimistic view of others comes naturally to the believing Latter-day Saint. Every person they will ever meet is a child of God—their brother or their sister in fact, not as a pleasant metaphor. Every person they meet, whatever their condition in this life, has been redeemed by the loving sacrifice of the Savior of the world. Every person who is accountable can exercise faith in Jesus Christ unto repentance, make and keep covenants, and qualify for eternal life, the life that God lives. Even those who are not accountable here will someday have that same potential.

With this as our reality, it is not hard to feel that the needs of those around us are as important as our own or that the most humble person has divine potential. Such thinking will lead not only to kindness and to generous appraisal of potential but to high expectations for each other. Sometimes the greatest kindness we could receive would be to have someone expect more from us than we do, because they see more clearly our divine heritage.

Here is one more characteristic: the great learner expects resistance and overcomes it. You remember from your early school days reading about the number of materials Thomas Edison tried in his search for a filament for an electric light bulb. The persistence he needed to work through failure after failure was an application of the rule of learning, not an exception to it.

That has been your experience as well. Some learning has been easy for you. But more often your enemy has been discouragement. You may try to avoid that by choosing to learn only what is easy for you, looking for the path of least resistance. But the great learner expects difficulty as part of learning and is determined to work through it.

That is a view common to believing Latter-day Saints. You may have been blessed by a mother as I was for whom the plan of salvation was reality. More than once I complained about some difficulty in my school days. Her answer, given in a matter-of-fact tone, was, "Hal, what else did you expect? Life is a test." Then she'd go off to something else and leave

> *Sometimes the greatest kindness we could receive would be to have someone expect more from us than we do, because they see more clearly our divine heritage.*

me to ponder. She knew that, because I understood the plan, her statement of the obvious would give me hope, not discouragement.

I knew and she knew that to have the blessings of Abraham, Isaac, and Jacob we need to face and pass comparable tests. She knew and I knew that the greater the test, the greater the compliment from a loving Heavenly Father.

She died after a decade of suffering with cancer. At her funeral President Spencer W. Kimball said something like this: "Some of you may wonder what great sins Mildred committed to explain her having to endure such suffering. It had nothing to do with sin. It was that her Heavenly Father wanted to polish her a little more."

I remember as I sat there at the time wondering what trials might lie ahead for me if a woman that good could be blessed by that much hard polishing.

You and I will face difficulty in our studies and in our lives, and we expect it because of what we know about who God is and that we are His children, what His hopes are for us, and how much He loves us. He will give us no test without preparing the way for us to pass it. Because of what we know about adversity in learning, in this community of Saints we pay special honor to determined learners because we know the price that they gladly pay. And we know from whence their power to persist through difficulty comes.

> *In this community we know that we are the brothers and sisters of Job, of Joseph in Egypt, of Joseph in Carthage Jail, and of Jesus in Gethsemane and on Golgotha's hill. So we are not surprised when sorrows come. We respect their place and know their potential.*

In this community we know that we are the brothers and sisters of Job, of Joseph in Egypt, of Joseph in Carthage Jail, and of Jesus in Gethsemane and on Golgotha's hill. So we are not surprised when sorrows come. We respect their place and know their potential.

You might well wonder what I would hope will come from this brief review of the power of our faith in the plan of salvation to produce humility and the power to learn. It is not that we will now go out to seek some grand experience to transform our lives and our learning.

The way to grow in the faith that we are the children of our Heavenly Father is to act like it. The time to start is now. When you receive some prompting in your heart about what God would have you do, or do differently, do what you have been prompted to do. Do it now. After you obey you will receive more impressions from God about what He requires of you. Keeping commandments increases the power to keep other commandments.

Today you could seek correction. You could keep a commitment. You could work hard. You could help someone else. You could plow through adversity. And as we do those things day after day, by and by we will find that we have learned whatever God would teach us for this life and for the next, with Him.

You are a child of God. Our Heavenly Father lives. Jesus is the Christ, our Savior. Through Joseph Smith the knowledge of the plan of salvation was restored. If we act upon that plan as we should, it will allow us to claim eternal life, which is our inheritance. And if we act upon it, we will be blessed with a humility that gives us the power to learn and the power to serve and the power to rise up to the privileges that God wants to grant us.

TRUST IN GOD,
THEN GO AND DO

The needs of Latter-day Saints across the world are great and varied. Each of you is a unique child of God. God knows you individually. He sends messages of encouragement, correction, and direction fitted to you and to your needs.

One day, as I was pondering and praying about how I might help meet these needs, I received an answer to my prayer as I read the words of Alma, a great servant of the Lord in the Book of Mormon:

"O that I were an angel, and could have the wish of mine heart, that I might go forth and speak with the trump of God, with a voice to shake the earth, and cry repentance unto every people!

"Yea, I would declare unto every soul, as with the voice of thunder, repentance and the plan of redemption, that they should repent and come unto our God, that there might not be more sorrow upon all the face of the earth.

"But behold, I am a man, and do sin in my wish; for I ought to be content with the things which the Lord hath allotted unto me" (Alma 29:1–3).

And then I found in Alma's reflection the direction for which I had been praying: "For behold, the Lord doth grant unto all nations, of their own nation and tongue, to teach his word, yea, in wisdom, all that he seeth fit that they should have; therefore we see that the Lord doth counsel in wisdom, according to that which is just and true" (Alma 29:8).

God sends messages and authorized messengers to His children. We need to develop enough trust in God and His servants that we will go out and obey His counsel. He wants that because He loves us and wants our happiness. And He knows how a lack of trust in Him brings sadness.

That lack of trust has brought sorrow to Heavenly Father's children from before the world was created. We know through the revelations of God to the Prophet Joseph Smith that many of our brothers and sisters in the premortal world rejected the plan for our mortal life presented by our Heavenly Father and His eldest Son, Jehovah (see Doctrine and Covenants 29:36–37; Abraham 3:27–28).

We need to develop enough trust in God and His servants that we will go out and obey His counsel. He wants that because He loves us and wants our happiness. And He knows how a lack of trust in Him brings sadness.

We don't know all the reasons for Lucifer's terrible success in inciting that rebellion. However, one reason is clear. Those who lost the blessing of coming into mortality lacked sufficient trust in God to avoid eternal misery.

The sad pattern of lack of trust in God has persisted since the Creation. I will be careful in giving examples from the lives of God's children since I do not know all the reasons for their lack of faith enough to trust Him. Many of you have studied the moments of crisis in their lives.

Jonah, for instance, not only rejected the message from the Lord to go to Nineveh but went the other way. Naaman could not trust the direction of the Lord's prophet to bathe in a river to allow the Lord to heal his leprosy, feeling the simple task was beneath his dignity.

The Savior invited Peter to leave the safety of a boat to walk to Him across water. We ache for him and see our own need for greater trust in God as we hear the account:

"And in the fourth watch of the night Jesus went unto them, walking on the sea.

"And when the disciples saw him walking on the sea, they were troubled, saying, It is a spirit; and they cried out for fear.

"But straightway Jesus spake unto them, saying, Be of good cheer; it is I; be not afraid.

"And Peter answered him and said, Lord, if it be thou, bid me come unto thee on the water.

"And he said, Come. And when Peter was come down out of the ship, he walked on the water, to go to Jesus.

"But when he saw the wind boisterous, he was afraid; and beginning to sink, he cried, saying, Lord, save me.

"And immediately Jesus stretched forth his hand, and caught him, and said unto him, O thou of little faith, wherefore didst thou doubt?" (Matthew 14:25–31).

We can take courage from the fact that Peter came to trust the Lord enough to stay faithful in His service all the way to his martyrdom.

The young Nephi in the Book of Mormon stirs in us a desire to develop trust in the Lord to obey His commandments, however hard they appear to us. Nephi faced danger and possible death when he said these words of trust that we can and must feel steadily in our hearts: "I will go and do the things which the Lord hath commanded, for I know that the Lord giveth no command-ments unto the children of men, save he shall prepare a way for them that they may accomplish the thing which he commandeth them" (1 Nephi 3:7).

That trust comes from knowing God. More than any other people on earth, we have, through the glorious events of the Restoration of the gospel, felt the peace that the Lord offered His people with the words "Be still, and know that I am God" (Psalm 46:10). My heart is filled with gratitude for what God has revealed about Himself that we might trust Him.

> *My heart is filled with gratitude for what God has revealed about Himself that we might trust Him.*

For me it began in 1820 with a young boy in a grove of trees on a farm in the state of New York. The boy, Joseph Smith Jr., walked among the trees to a secluded spot. He knelt to pray with complete trust that God would answer his pleading to know what he should do to be cleansed and saved through the Atonement of Jesus Christ (see *Teachings of Presidents of the Church: Joseph Smith* [2007], 28).

Each time I read his account, my trust in God and His servants expands:

"I saw a pillar of light exactly over my head, above the bright-ness of the sun, which descended gradually until it fell upon me.

"It no sooner appeared than I found myself delivered from the enemy which held me bound. When the light rested upon me I saw two Personages, whose brightness and glory defy all descrip-tion, standing above me in the air. One of them spake unto me, calling me by name and said, pointing to the other—*This is My Beloved Son. Hear Him!*" (Joseph Smith–History 1:16–17).

The Father revealed to us that He lives, that Jesus Christ is His Beloved Son, and that He loved us enough to send that Son to save us, who are His children. And because I have a testimony that He called that unlettered boy as an apostle and prophet, I trust His apostles and prophets today and those they call to serve God.

That trust has blessed my life and the lives of my family. Years ago I heard President Ezra Taft Benson counsel us to do all we could to get out of debt and stay out. He mentioned mortgages on houses. He said that it might not be possible, but it would be best if we could pay off all our mortgage debt (see, for example, "Prepare for the Days of Tribulation," *Ensign,* November 1980, 33).

I turned to my wife after the meeting and asked, "Do you think there is any way we could do that?" At first we couldn't. And then by evening I thought of a property we had acquired in another state. For years we had tried to sell it without success.

But because we trusted God and a few words from the midst of His servant's message, we placed a phone call Monday morning to the man in San Francisco who had our property listed to sell. I had called him a few weeks before, and he had said then, "We haven't had anyone show interest in your property for years."

But on the Monday after conference, I heard an answer that to this day strengthens my trust in God and His servants.

The man on the phone said, "I am surprised by your call. A man came in today inquiring whether he could buy your property." In amazement I asked, "How much did he offer to pay?" It was a few dollars more than the amount of our mortgage.

A person might say that was only a coincidence. But our mortgage was paid off. And our family still listens for any word in a prophet's message that might be sent to tell what we should do to find the security and peace God wants for us.

Such trust in God can bless communities as well as families. I grew up in a small town in New Jersey. Our branch of the Church had fewer than twenty members who regularly attended.

Among them was a woman—an older, very humble convert to the Church. She was an immigrant who spoke with a heavy Norwegian accent. She was the only member of the Church in her family and the only member of the Church in the city in which she lived.

Through my father, who was the branch president, the Lord called her as the president of the branch Relief Society. She had no handbook to tell her what to do. No other member of the Church lived near her. She only knew

Our family listens for any word in a prophet's message that might be sent to tell what we should do to find the security and peace God wants for us.

that the Lord cared for those in need and the few words in the motto of the Relief Society: "Charity never faileth."

It was in the depths of what we now call the Great Depression. Thousands were out of work and homeless. So, feeling she had her errand from the Lord, she asked her neighbors for old clothes. She washed the clothes, pressed them, and put them in cardboard boxes on her back porch. When men without money needed clothes and asked her neighbors for help, they would say, "Go to the house down the street. There is a Mormon lady living there who will give you what you need."

The Lord did not run the city, but He changed a part of it for the better. He called one tiny woman—alone—who trusted Him enough to find out what He wanted her to do and then did it. Because of her trust in the Lord, she was able to help in that city hundreds of Heavenly Father's children in need.

That same trust in God can bless nations. I have come to know that we can trust God to fulfill the promise of Alma that "behold, the Lord doth grant unto all nations, of their own nation and tongue, to teach his word, yea, in wisdom, all that he seeth fit that they should have" (Alma 29:8).

God does not rule in nations, but He is mindful of them. He can and does place people in positions of influence who want what is best for the people and who trust in the Lord (see 2 Chronicles 36:22–23; Ezra 1:1–3; Isaiah 45:1, 13).

> *God does not rule in nations, but He is mindful of them. He can and does place people in positions of influence who want what is best for the people and who trust in the Lord.*

I have seen it in my travels across the world. In a city of more than ten million people, I spoke to the Latter-day Saints gathered by the thousands in conference. It was held in a large sports arena.

Before the meeting began, I noticed a handsome young man sitting on the front row. He was surrounded by others who, like him, were better dressed than most of those around them. I asked the General Authority of the Church near me who the men were. He whispered that it was the mayor of the city and his staff.

As I walked to my car after the meeting, I was surprised to see the mayor waiting to greet me, flanked by his staff. He stepped forward, extended his hand to me, and said, "I thank you for coming to our city and to our country. We are grateful for what you do to build up your people. With such people and such families, we could create the harmony and the prosperity we want for our people."

I saw in that moment that he was one of the honest in heart

placed by God in power among His children. We are a tiny minority among the citizens of that great city and nation. The mayor knew little of our doctrine and few of our people. Yet God had sent him the message that Latter-day Saints, under covenant to trust God and His authorized servants, would become a light to his people.

I know that the servants of God whom we sustain as prophets, seers, and revelators are called of God to give messages to His children. The Lord has said of them: "What I the Lord have spoken, I have spoken, and I excuse not myself; and though the heavens and the earth pass away, my word shall not pass away, but shall all be fulfilled, whether by mine own voice or by the voice of my servants, it is the same" (Doctrine and Covenants 1:38).

You show your trust in Him when you listen with the intent to learn and repent and then you go and do whatever He asks. If you trust God enough to listen for His message in every sermon, song, and prayer you hear in your Church meetings, you will find it. And if you then go and do what He would have you do, your power to trust Him will grow, and in time you will be overwhelmed with gratitude to find that He has come to trust you.

If you trust God enough to listen for His message in every sermon, song, and prayer you hear in your Church meetings, you will find it. And if you then go and do what He would have you do, your power to trust Him will grow, and in time you will be overwhelmed with gratitude to find that He has come to trust you.

BE READY

Wherever I am in the day or night, there is nearby a small container of olive oil. There is one that I keep in the middle drawer of the desk where I work. There is one in my pocket when I am working outdoors or traveling. There is also one in the kitchen cabinet in my home.

Each of these containers has a date on it. It is the day when someone exercised the power of the priesthood to consecrate the pure oil for the healing of the sick.

Perhaps you might think that I am a little extreme in my preparation. But the call during the day or the knock at the door at night always comes as a surprise. Someone will say, "Please, could you come quickly?" Once, years ago, it was a father calling from a hospital. His three-year-old daughter had been thrown fifty feet by a speeding car as she ran across the street to join her mother. When I arrived at the hospital, the father pled that the power of the priesthood would preserve her life. The doctors and the nurses only reluctantly let us reach through a plastic barrier to place a drop of oil on the one opening in the heavy bandages which covered her head. A doctor said to me, with irritation in his voice, "Hurry with whatever you are going to do. She is dying."

He was wrong. She lived, and contrary to what the doctor had said, she not only lived, but she learned to walk again.

When the call came, I was ready. The preparation was far more than having consecrated oil close at hand. It must begin long before the crisis which requires priesthood power. Those who are prepared will be ready to answer.

The preparation begins in families, in Aaronic Priesthood quorums, and mostly in the private lives of young men. The quorums and the families must help, but the preparation that counts will be made by the young men making choices to rise to their great destiny as priesthood servants for God.

The destiny of the rising generation of priesthood holders is far more than to be ready to bring God's power down to heal the sick. The preparation is to be ready to go and do whatever the Lord wants done as the world is preparing for His coming.

The destiny of the rising generation of priesthood holders is far more than to be ready to bring God's power down to heal the sick. The preparation is to be ready to go and do whatever the Lord wants done as the world is preparing for His coming. None of us knows exactly what those errands will be. But we know what it will take to be ready, so each of us can prepare.

What you will need in the dramatic moment will be built in the steady performance of obedient service. I will tell you two of the things you will need and the preparation it takes to be ready.

The first is to have faith. The priesthood is the authority to act in the name of God. It is the right to call down the powers of heaven. So you must have faith that God lives and that you have won His confidence to allow you to use His power for His purposes.

An instance from the Book of Mormon will help you see how one man made that preparation. There was a priesthood holder named Nephi who received a hard assignment from the Lord. He was sent by God to call wicked people to repentance before it was too late for them. In their wickedness and hatred, they were killing each other. Even their sorrow had not humbled them enough to repent and obey God.

Because of Nephi's preparation, God blessed him with power to fulfill his assignment. In His loving and empowering words to Nephi, there is a guide for us:

"Blessed art thou, Nephi, for those things which thou hast done; for I have beheld how thou hast with unwearyingness declared the word, which I have given unto thee, unto this people. And thou hast not feared them, and hast not sought thine own life, but hast sought my will, and to keep my commandments.

"And now, because thou hast done this with such unwearyingness, behold, I will bless thee forever; and I will make thee mighty in word and in deed, in faith and in works; yea, even that all things shall be done unto thee according to thy word, for thou shalt not ask that which is contrary to my will.

"Behold, thou art Nephi, and I am God. Behold, I declare it unto thee in the presence of mine angels, that ye shall have power over this people, and shall smite the earth with famine, and with pestilence, and destruction, according to the wickedness of this people.

"Behold, I give unto you power, that whatsoever ye shall seal on earth shall be sealed in heaven; and whatsoever ye shall loose on earth shall be loosed in heaven; and thus shall ye have power among this people" (Helaman 10:4–7).

As the account from the Book of Mormon tells us, the people did not repent. So Nephi asked God to change the seasons. He asked for a miracle to help the people choose to repent because of famine. The famine came. The people repented, and then they begged Nephi to have God send rain. He did ask God, and God honored his unshakable faith.

That faith did not come in the moment when Nephi needed it, nor did God's trust in Nephi. He earned that great faith and God's confidence by courageous and sustained labor in the Lord's service. You young men are building that faith now for the days ahead when you will need it.

Faith did not come in the moment when Nephi needed it, nor did God's trust in Nephi. He earned that great faith and God's confidence by courageous and sustained labor in the Lord's service.

It may be so small a thing as to keep careful minutes in a deacons or a teachers quorum. There were young men years ago who kept meticulous records of what was decided and what was done by boys only months older than they were. That took faith that God called even twelve-year-olds into His service who were being guided by revelation. Some of those quorum secretaries of long ago now sit in the presiding councils of the Church. They now read the minutes others prepare. And revelation flows to them now as it did to the leaders they served when they were boys like you. They had been prepared to trust that God reveals His *will,* even in apparently small matters, in His kingdom.

Now, the Lord said Nephi could be trusted because he would ask nothing contrary to God's will. To have that confidence in

Nephi, the Lord had to be sure that Nephi believed in revelation, sought it, and followed it. Long experience following inspiration from God was a part of Nephi's priesthood preparation. It must be part of yours.

I see that happening today. In recent months I have heard deacons, teachers, and priests give talks which are clearly as inspired and powerful as you will hear in a general conference. As I have felt the power being given to young holders of the priesthood, I have thought that the rising generation is rising around us, as if on an incoming tide. My prayer is that those of us in the generations which have come before will rise on the tide with them. The preparation of the Aaronic Priesthood is a blessing to us all as well as to those they will serve in their generation and the generations to follow.

Yet all is not perfect in Zion. Not all of the youth choose to prepare. That choice must be their own. They are responsible for themselves. That is the Lord's way in His loving plan. But many young men have little or no support from those who could help as they prepare. Those of us who can help will be held accountable by the Lord. A father who neglects or interferes with a son's development of faith or his ability to follow inspiration will someday know sorrow. That will be true for anyone placed in a position to help these young men choose wisely and well in their days in the preparatory priesthood.

Now, the second thing they will need is confidence that they can live up to the blessings and the trust which God has offered them. Most of the influences around them drag them down to doubt the existence of God, of His love for them, and of the reality of the sometimes quiet messages they receive through the Holy Ghost and the Spirit of Christ. Their peers may urge them to choose sin. If young men choose sin, those messages from God will become more faint.

We can help them choose to prepare by loving them, by warning them, and by showing confidence in them. But we can help them even more by our example of a faithful and inspired servant. In our families, in quorums, in classes, and as we associate with them in any setting, we can act as true priesthood holders who use its power as God has taught us.

We can help youth choose to prepare by loving them, by warning them, and by showing confidence in them. But we can help them even more by our example of a faithful and inspired servant.

For me, that instruction is most clear in the 121st section of the Doctrine and Covenants. The Lord warns us in that section to have our motives pure: "No power or influence can or ought to be maintained by virtue of the priesthood, only by persuasion, by long-suffering, by gentleness and meekness, and by love unfeigned" (Doctrine and Covenants 121:41). As we lead and influence young men, we must never do it to gratify our pride or our ambition. We must never use compulsion in any degree of unrighteousness. That is a high standard of the example we must set for our youth.

I saw it done when I was a teacher and a priest. My bishop and those who served under him were determined not to lose even one of us. As nearly as I could see, their determination was motivated by love for the Lord and for us, not for any selfish purpose.

The bishop had a system. Every adviser of every quorum was to contact every young man he had not spoken to that Sunday.

They were not to go to bed until they had either talked to the boy who had been missing, to his parents, or to a close friend. The bishop promised them that he would not turn out his light until he had heard a report about every boy. I don't think he gave them an order. He simply made it clear that he did not expect their lights to go out until they had given that report.

He and those who served under him were doing far more than watching over us. They were showing us by example what it means to care for the Lord's sheep. No effort was too much for him or for those who served us in our quorums. By their example, they taught us what it means to be unwearying in the Lord's service. The Lord was preparing us by example.

I have no idea whether they thought any one of us was going to be anything special. But they treated us as if they did by being willing to pay any personal price to keep us from losing faith.

I don't know how the bishop got so many people to have such high expectations. As nearly as I can tell, it was done "by persuasion, by long-suffering, by gentleness and meekness, and by love unfeigned." The "no lights out" method the bishop used would not work in some places. But the example of unwavering care for every young man and reaching out quickly brought the power of heaven into our lives. It always will. It helped young men prepare for the days when God needed them in families and in His kingdom.

My father was an example for me of what the Lord teaches in the 121st section about getting heaven's help in preparing young men. During my early years, he was sometimes disappointed by my performance. He let me know it. Hearing his voice, I could feel he thought I was better than that. But he did it in the Lord's way: "Reproving betimes with sharpness, when moved upon by the Holy Ghost; and then showing forth afterwards an increase of love toward him whom thou hast reproved, lest he esteem thee to be his enemy" (Doctrine and Covenants 121:43).

I knew, even after the most direct correction, that Dad's reproof was given in love. In fact, his love seemed to increase when he used even his strongest correction, which was a disapproving and disappointed look. He was my leader and my trainer, never using compulsory means, and I am sure that the promise given in the Doctrine and Covenants will be fulfilled for him. His influence on me will flow unto him "forever and ever" (Doctrine and Covenants 121:46).

Many fathers and leaders, when they hear the words of the 121st section of the Doctrine and Covenants, will feel that they must rise higher to come up to that standard. I do. Can you remember a moment when you rebuked a child or youth with sharpness when you were moved by something other than inspiration? Can you remember a time when you told a son to do something or make a sacrifice you were not willing to do or make yourself? Those feelings of regret can spur us to repentance to become more nearly the examples we have covenanted to be.

I knew, even after the most direct correction, that Dad's reproof was given in love. In fact, his love seemed to increase when he used even his strongest correction.

As we meet our obligations as fathers and leaders, we will help the next generation rise to their glorious future. They will be better than we are, just as you have tried to be even better parents than your parents and better leaders than the great ones who helped you.

It is my prayer that we will be determined to do better every day to prepare the rising generation. Each time I see a bottle of consecrated oil, I will remember the feeling I have of wanting to do more to help young men prepare for their days of service and opportunity. I pray for a blessing of preparation for them. I am confident that, with the Lord's help and ours, they will be ready.

"Man Down!"

Ours is not a time of peace. That has been so since Satan arrayed his forces against our Heavenly Father's plan in the premortal existence. We don't know the details of the combat then. But we know one result. Satan and his followers were cast down into the earth. And since the creation of Adam and Eve, the conflict has continued. We have seen it intensify. And the scriptures suggest that the war will become more violent and the spiritual casualties on the Lord's side will mount.

Almost all of us have seen a battlefield portrayed in a film or read the description in a story. Over the din of explosions and the shouts of soldiers, there comes a cry, "Man down!"

When that cry sounds, faithful fellow soldiers will move toward the sound. Another soldier or a medic will ignore danger and move to the injured comrade. And the man down will know that help will come. Whatever the risk, someone will run low or crawl to get there in time to protect and give aid. That is true in every band of men joined in a difficult and dangerous mission which they are determined to fulfill at any sacrifice. The histories of such groups are full of stories of those loyal men who were determined that no man would be left behind.

Here is one instance from an official account (see *The U.S. Army Leadership Field Manual* [2004], 28–29). During fighting in

Somalia in October of 1993, two United States Army Rangers in a helicopter during the firefight learned that two other helicopters near them had fallen to the earth. The two rangers, in their relative safety aloft, learned by radio that no ground forces were available to rescue one of the downed aircrews. Growing numbers of the enemy were closing in on the crash site.

The two men watching from above volunteered to go down to the ground (the words they used on the radio were to "be inserted") to protect their critically wounded comrades. Their request was denied because the situation was so dangerous. They asked a second time. Permission was again denied. Only after their third request were they put down on the ground.

Armed only with their personal weapons, they fought their way to the crashed helicopter and the injured fliers. They moved through intense small-arms fire as enemies converged on the crash site. They pulled the wounded from the wreckage. They put themselves in a perimeter around the wounded, placing themselves in the most dangerous positions. They protected their comrades until their ammunition was depleted and they were fatally wounded. Their bravery and their sacrifice saved the life of a pilot who would have been lost.

They were each awarded posthumously the Medal of Honor, their nation's highest recognition for bravery in the face of an armed enemy. The citation reads that what they did was "above and beyond the call of duty."

But I wonder if they saw it that way as they moved to the downed airmen. Out of loyalty they felt a duty to stand by their fellow soldiers, whatever the cost. The courage to act and their selfless service came from feeling that they were responsible for the lives, the happiness, and the safety of comrades.

Such a feeling of responsibility for others is at the heart of faithful priesthood service. Our comrades are being wounded in the spiritual conflict around us. So are the people we are called to serve and protect from harm. Spiritual wounds are not easily visible, except with inspired eyes. But bishops, branch presidents, and mission presidents sitting before fellow disciples of the Savior can see the wounded and the wounds.

It has happened for years and across the earth. I remember as a bishop looking out at the face and the posture of a young man of the priesthood and having the thought come to my mind so clearly that it seemed audible: "I need to see him—and soon. Something is happening. He needs help."

The wounds of sin are often not felt at first by the one being hurt. Satan seems sometimes to inject something to deaden the spiritual pain while inflicting the wound. Unless something happens soon to begin repentance, the wound can worsen and widen.

I would never put off such an impression because I had learned that the wounds of sin are often not felt at first by the one being hurt. Satan seems sometimes to inject something to deaden the spiritual pain while inflicting the wound. Unless something happens soon to begin repentance, the wound can worsen and widen.

Consequently, as a priesthood holder responsible for the spiritual survival of some of Heavenly Father's children, you will then move to help without waiting for a cry, "Man down!" Even a best friend or other leaders or parents may not see what you have seen.

You may have been the only one to sense by inspiration the warning cry. The others may feel, as you will be tempted to think,

"Maybe the trouble I thought I saw is just my imagination. What right do I have to judge another? It's not my responsibility. I'll leave it alone until he asks for help."

Only an authorized judge in Israel is given the power and the responsibility to verify that there is a serious wound, to explore it, and then, under inspiration from God, to prescribe the necessary treatment for healing to begin. Yet you are under covenant to go to a spiritually wounded child of God. You are responsible to be brave enough and bold enough not to turn away.

You are under covenant to go to a spiritually wounded child of God. You are responsible to be brave enough and bold enough not to turn away.

I need to explain, as best I can, at least two things. First, why do you have a responsibility to move to help your wounded friend? And, second, how do you meet that responsibility?

First, you are under covenant, as has been made clear to you, that when you accepted the trust from God to receive the priesthood, you accepted a responsibility for whatever you might do or fail to do for the salvation of others however difficult and dangerous that might appear to be for you.

There are countless examples of priesthood holders who shouldered that grave responsibility as you and I must. This is how Jacob in the Book of Mormon described his sacred trust when he moved in difficult circumstances to give aid: "Now, my beloved brethren, I, Jacob, according to the responsibility which I am under to God, to magnify mine office with soberness, and that I might rid my garments of your sins, I come up into the temple this day that I might declare unto you the word of God" (Jacob 2:2).

Now, you might object that Jacob was a prophet and you are not. But your office, whatever it is in the priesthood, brings with it an obligation to "lift up the hands which hang down, and strengthen the feeble knees" of those around you (Doctrine and Covenants 81:5). You are the Lord's servant covenanted to do for others, as best you can, what He would do.

Your great opportunity and your responsibility are described in Ecclesiastes:

"Two are better than one; because they have a good reward for their labour.

"For if they fall, the one will lift up his fellow: but woe to him that is alone when he falleth; for he hath not another to help him up" (Ecclesiastes 4:9–10).

From that, you will understand the true and sobering words from Joseph Smith: "None but fools will trifle with the souls of men" (*History of the Church of Jesus Christ of Latter-day Saints*, 7 vols. [1932–1951], 3:295). As Jacob believed, the woe of any fallen man or woman he could have helped and did not would become his own sorrow. Your happiness and that of those you are called to serve as a priesthood holder are bound together.

Now, we come to the question of how best to help those you are called to serve and rescue. That will depend on your capacities and on the nature of your priesthood relationship to the person who is in spiritual peril. Let me give three cases which may be your opportunity at times in your priesthood service.

Let's start when you are an inexperienced junior companion, a teacher in the Aaronic Priesthood assigned with a seasoned companion to visit a young family. Before preparing for the visit you will pray for strength and inspiration to see their needs and know what help you could give. If you can, you will have that prayer with your companion, naming those you will visit. As you pray your heart will be drawn out to them personally and to God. You and your companion will agree on what you hope to accomplish. You will work out a plan for what you will do.

Whatever the plan, you will watch and listen with great intensity and humility during the visit. You are young and inexperienced. But the Lord knows their spiritual state and their needs perfectly. He loves them. And because you know He sends you to act for Him, you can have faith that you can sense their needs and what you can do to meet your charge to help. It will come as you visit face-to-face in their home. That is why you have this priesthood charge in the Doctrine and Covenants: "Visit the house of each member, and exhort them to pray vocally and in secret and attend to all family duties" (Doctrine and Covenants 20:47).

And then you have an added charge which takes even greater discernment:

"The teacher's duty is to watch over the church always, and be with and strengthen them;

"And see that there is no iniquity in the church, neither hardness with each other, neither lying, backbiting, nor evil speaking;

"And see that the church meet together often, and also see that all the members do their duty" (Doctrine and Covenants 20:53–55).

You and your companion will rarely receive inspiration to know the details of the degree to which they are meeting that standard. But I can promise you from experience that you will be given the gift to know what is well with them. And from that you will be able to encourage them. There is another promise I can make: you and your companion will be inspired to know what changes they could make to begin the spiritual healing they need. The words of what you are charged to have happen in their lives will almost certainly contain some of the most important changes the Lord would have them make.

If your companion feels an impression to urge change, watch what he does. You will likely be surprised at the way the Spirit guides him to speak. There will be the sound of love in his voice. He will find a way to tie the needed change with a blessing that will follow. If it is the father or mother who needs to make a change, he may show how it would lead to happiness for the children. He will describe the change as a move away from unhappiness to a better and safer place.

Your contribution during the visit may seem to you small, but it can be more powerful than you may think possible. You will show by your face and manner that you care for the people. They will see that your love for them and the Lord makes you unafraid. And you will be bold enough to bear your testimony to truth. Your humble, simple, and perhaps brief testimony may touch the heart of a person more easily than that of your more experienced companion. I have seen it happen.

Your humble, simple, and perhaps brief testimony may touch the heart of a person more easily than that of your more experienced companion. I have seen it happen.

Whatever part you play in that priesthood visit, your desire to go to the people for the Lord to help them will bring at least two blessings. First, you will feel the love of God for the people you visit. And, second, you will feel the Savior's gratitude for your desire to give the help the Savior knew they needed.

He sent you to them because He trusted that you would

go feeling responsible to urge them toward Him and toward happiness.

As you grow a little older, there is another opportunity which will come to you in priesthood service. You will come to know your fellow quorum members well. You may have played basketball or football or shared some youth activities and service projects. With some you will have become close friends.

You will have come to recognize when they are happy and when they are sad. Neither of you may be in a position of authority in the quorum. But you will feel responsible for your fellow member in the priesthood. He may confide in you that he is beginning to break a commandment which you know will do him spiritual harm. He may ask for advice because he trusts you.

I can tell you from experience that if you succeed in influencing him away from a dangerous path, you will never forget the joy which came from being his true friend. If you do not succeed, I promise that when his grief and sadness come, as they will, you will feel his pain as if it were your own. Yet if you tried to help, you will still be his friend. And, in fact, for years he may talk with you about what good things there might have been and how grateful he is that you cared enough to try. You will comfort him then and invite him again, as you did in your youth, to come back to the happiness which the Atonement still makes possible for him.

Now, later in your life you will be a father—a priesthood father. What you have learned in your priesthood service as you helped others away from sadness and toward happiness will give you the power you will need and want. Years of being responsible for the souls of men will prepare you for helping and protecting your family, whom you will love more than you can imagine in your youth. You will know how to lead them with priesthood power to safety.

My prayer is that you will have joy in your priesthood service throughout your life and forever. I pray that you will develop the bravery and love for Heavenly Father's children that led the sons of Mosiah to plead for the chance to face death and danger to take the gospel to a hardened people. Their desire and their bravery came from feeling responsible for the eternal happiness of strangers in danger of eternal misery (see Mosiah 28:1–8).

May we have a part of the desire which Jehovah had, in the world before this one, when He asked to come down from the realms of glory to serve us and give His life for us. He asked His Father, "Send me" (Abraham 3:27).

Years of being responsible for the souls of men will prepare you for helping and protecting your family, whom you will love more than you can imagine in your youth. You will know how to lead them with priesthood power to safety.

I testify that you were called of God and you are sent to serve His children. He wants that no one be left behind. God will give you inspiration and strength to meet your charge to help His children find their way to the happiness made possible by the Atonement of Jesus Christ.

STRENGTH IN ADVERSITY

ADVERSITY

With all the differences in our lives, we have at least one challenge in common. We all must deal with adversity. There may be periods, sometimes long ones, when our lives seem to flow with little difficulty. But it is in the nature of our being human that comfort gives way to distress, periods of good health come to an end, and misfortunes arrive. Particularly when the comfortable times have gone on for a while, the arrival of suffering or the loss of material security can bring fear and sometimes even anger.

The anger comes at least in part from a feeling that what is happening is unfair. The good health and the serene sense of being secure can come to seem deserved and natural. When they vanish, a feeling of injustice can come. Even a brave man I knew wept and cried out in his physical suffering to those who ministered to him: "I have always tried to be good. How could this happen?"

That aching for an answer to "How could this happen?" becomes even more painful when those struggling include those we love. And it is especially hard for us to accept when those afflicted seem to us to be blameless. Then the distress can shake faith in the reality of a loving and all-powerful God. Some of us have seen such doubt come to infect a whole generation of people in times of war or famine. Such doubt can grow and spread until some may turn away from God, whom they charge with being indifferent or cruel.

And if unchecked, those feelings can lead to loss of faith that there is a God at all.

I want to assure you that our Heavenly Father and the Savior live and that They love all humanity. The very opportunity for us to face adversity and affliction is part of the evidence of Their infinite love. God gave us the gift of living in mortality so that we could be prepared to receive the greatest of all the gifts of God, which is eternal life. Then our spirits will be changed. We will become able to want what God wants, to think as He thinks, and thus be prepared for the trust of an endless posterity to teach and to lead through tests to be raised up to qualify to live forever in eternal life.

> *I want to assure you that our Heavenly Father and the Savior live and that They love all humanity. The very opportunity for us to face adversity and affliction is part of the evidence of Their infinite love.*

It is clear that for us to have that gift and to be given that trust, we must be transformed through making righteous choices where that is hard to do. We are prepared for so great a trust by passing through trying and testing experiences in mortality. That education can come only as we are subject to trials while serving God and others for Him.

In this education we experience misery and happiness, sickness and health, the sadness from sin and the joy of forgiveness. That forgiveness can come only through the infinite Atonement of the Savior, which He worked out through pain we could not bear and which we can only faintly comprehend.

I have seen faith and courage come from a testimony that it

is true that we are being prepared for eternal life. The Lord will rescue His faithful disciples. And the disciple who accepts a trial as an invitation to grow and therefore qualify for eternal life can find peace in the midst of the struggle.

I spoke recently to a young father who has lost his job in the recent economic crisis. He knows that hundreds of thousands of people with exactly his skills are looking desperately for work to feed their families. His quiet confidence led me to ask him what he had done to become so confident that he would find a way to support his family. He said he had examined his life to be sure that he had done all he could to be worthy of the Lord's help. It was clear that his need and his faith in Jesus Christ were leading him to be obedient to God's commandments when it is hard to do. He said that he saw that opportunity as he and his wife were reading in Alma where the Lord had prepared a people to find the gospel through adversity.

You remember the moment when Alma turned to the man who led the people in distress. The man told him that they had been persecuted and rejected for their poverty. And the record goes:

"And now when Alma heard this, he turned him about, his face immediately towards him, and he beheld with great joy; for he beheld that their afflictions had truly humbled them, and that they were in a preparation to hear the word.

"Therefore he did say no more to the other multitude; but he stretched forth his hand, and cried unto those whom he beheld, who were truly penitent, and said unto them:

"I behold that ye are lowly in heart; and if so, blessed are ye" (Alma 32:6–8).

The scripture goes on to praise those of us who prepared for adversity in the more prosperous times. Many of you had the faith to try to qualify for the help you now need, before the crisis came.

Alma continued, "Yea, he that truly humbleth himself, and repenteth of his sins, and endureth to the end, the same shall be blessed—yea, much more blessed than they who are compelled to be humble because of their exceeding poverty" (Alma 32:15).

That young man with whom I spoke recently was one who had done more than put away food and a little savings for the misfortune which living prophets had warned would come. He had begun to prepare his heart to be worthy of the Lord's help which he knew he would in the near future need. When I asked his wife on the day he lost his job if she was worried, she said with cheerfulness in her voice, "No, we've just come from the bishop's office. We are full-tithe payers." Now, it is still too early to tell, but I felt assured as they seemed to be assured: "Things will work out." Tragedy did not erode their faith; it tested it and strengthened it. And the feeling of peace the Lord has promised has already been delivered in the midst of the storm. Other miracles are sure to follow.

The Lord always suits the relief to the person in need to best strengthen and purify him or her. Often it will come in the inspiration to do what might seem especially hard for the person who needs help himself. One of the great trials of life is losing to death a beloved husband or wife. The Lord knows the needs of those separated from loved ones by death. He saw the pain of widows and knew of their needs from His earthly experience. He asked a beloved Apostle, from the agony of the cross, to care for His widowed mother, who would now lose a son. He now feels the needs of husbands who lose their wives and the needs of wives who are left alone by death.

Most of us know widows who need attention. What touches me is to hear, as I have, of an older widow whom I was intending to visit again having been inspired to visit a younger widow to comfort her. A widow needing comfort herself was sent to comfort another. The Lord helped and blessed two widows by inspiring them to encourage each other. So He gave succor to them both.

The Lord sent help in that same way to the humble poor in Alma 34 who had responded to the teaching and testimony of His servants. Once they had repented and were converted, they were still poor. But He sent them to do for others what they might reasonably have thought was beyond them and which they still needed. They were to give others what they would have hoped He would give them. Through His servant, the Lord gave these poor converts this hard task: "After ye have done all these things, if ye turn away the needy, and the naked, and visit not the sick and

The Lord always suits the relief to the person in need to best strengthen and purify him or her. Often it will come in the inspiration to do what might seem especially hard for the person who needs help himself.

afflicted, and impart of your substance, if ye have, to those who stand in need—I say unto you, if ye do not any of these things, behold, your prayer is vain, and availeth you nothing, and ye are as hypocrites who do deny the faith" (Alma 34:28).

That may seem much to ask of people in such great need themselves. But I know one young man who was inspired to do that very thing early in his marriage. He and his wife were barely getting by on a tiny budget. But he saw another couple even poorer than they were. To the surprise of his wife, he gave help to them from their scanty finances. A promised blessing of peace came while they were still in their poverty. The blessing of prosperity beyond their fondest dreams came later. And the pattern of seeing someone in need, someone with less or in pain, has never ceased.

There is yet another trial which, when endured well, can bring blessings in this life and blessings forever. Age and illness can test the best of us. My friend served as our bishop when my daughters were still at home. They speak of what they felt when he bore his simple testimony around campfires in the mountains. He loved them, and they knew it. He was released as our bishop. He had served as a bishop before in another state. Those I have met who were from his earlier ward remember him as my daughters do.

I visited him in his home from time to time to thank him and to give him priesthood blessings. His health began a slow decline. I can't remember all the ailments he suffered. He needed surgery. He was in constant pain. Yet every time I visited him to give him comfort, he turned the tables; I always was the one comforted. His back and legs forced him to use a cane to walk. Yet there he was in church, always sitting near the door, where he could greet those arriving early, with a smile.

I will never forget the feeling of wonder and admiration which came over me when I opened the back door at home and saw him coming up our driveway. It was the day we put out our garbage cans to be picked up by city workers. I had put the can out in the morning. But there he was dragging my garbage can up the hill with one hand while he balanced himself with a cane in his other hand. He was giving me the help he thought I needed when he needed it far more than I did. And he was helping with a smile and without being asked.

I visited him when he finally had to be cared for by nurses and doctors. He was lying in a hospital bed, still in pain and still smiling. His wife had called me to say that he was getting weaker. My son and I gave him a priesthood blessing as he lay in the bed with tubes and bottles connected to him. I sealed the blessing with a promise that he would have time and the strength to do all that God had for him to do in this life, to pass every test. He stretched out his hand to grasp mine as I stepped away from his bed to leave. I was surprised at the strength of his grip and the firmness in his voice when he said, "I'm going to make it."

I left thinking that I would see him again soon. But the phone call came within a day. He was gone to the glorious place where he will see the Savior, who is his perfect judge and will be ours. As I spoke at his funeral, I thought of the words of Paul when he knew that he would go to that place where my neighbor and friend has gone:

"But watch thou in all things, endure afflictions, do the work of an evangelist, make full proof of thy ministry.

"For I am now ready to be offered, and the time of my departure is at hand.

"I have fought a good fight, I have finished my course, I have kept the faith:

"Henceforth there is laid up for me a crown of righteousness, which the Lord, the righteous judge, shall give me at that day: and not to me only, but unto all them also that love his appearing" (2 Timothy 4:5–8).

I have confidence that my neighbor made it through his trial and will face his judge with a joyous smile.

I bear you my testimony that God the Father lives. He set a course for each of us that can polish and perfect us to be with Him. I testify that the Savior lives. His Atonement makes possible our being purified as we keep His commandments and our sacred covenants. And I know from my own experience that He can and will give us strength to rise through every trial.

FAITH OF OUR FATHERS

If I could visit with each of you and listen to the story of your life and what you know of your ancestors' lives, my guess is that we would discover great differences. Each life is unique. That struck me as I reread journals and histories that have been passed down through the generations, describing lives of people as diverse as that of Mary Bommeli, my great-grandmother, and of Wilford Woodruff, a prophet of God. Yet I see a thread of faith, a particular faith, running in the lives of those heroes of the Restoration whose steadfastness and courage leave us in awe. Perhaps if we examine that thread, we may find it in our own lives and strengthen it.

Those histories reveal as much about faith from what people did as from what they declared in words. Different as were their challenges and their responses, I thought I saw a recurring pattern. Here it is.

They shared a faith that the kingdom of God had been established for the last time, that it would triumph over great opposition and would become glorious in preparation for the day when the Savior would come to accept it, that it would stand forever, and that theirs was a rare privilege to have been called out of the world to build it.

They were sure that they were establishing Zion, a place of refuge. It is not surprising then that they pled for that Zion and that they expected not only to build it but to enjoy living in it. What is surprising is that their faith increased when they pleaded for Zion to be established even as they saw times of safety turn to times of testing.

Listen to the Prophet Joseph's pleadings in a letter from Kirtland to the exiled Saints in Missouri, December 10, 1833:

"Now hear the prayer of your unworthy brother in the new and everlasting covenant:—O My God! Thou who hast called and chosen a few, through Thy weak instrument, by commandment, and sent them to Missouri, a place which Thou didst call Zion, and commanded Thy servants to consecrate it unto Thyself for a place of refuge and safety for the gathering of Thy Saints, to be built up a holy city unto Thyself; and as Thou hast said that no other place should be appointed like unto this, therefore, I ask Thee in the name of Jesus Christ, to return Thy people unto their houses and their inheritances, to enjoy the fruit of their labors; that all the waste places may be built up; that all the enemies of Thy people, who will not repent and turn unto Thee may be destroyed from off the face of the land; and let a house be built and established unto Thy name; and let all the losses that Thy people have sustained, be rewarded unto them, even more than four-fold, that the borders of Zion may be enlarged forever; and let her be established no more to be thrown down; and let all thy Saints, when they are scattered, as sheep, and are persecuted, flee unto Zion, and be established in the midst of her; and let her be organized according to Thy law; and let this prayer ever be recorded before Thy face. Give Thy Holy Spirit unto my brethren, unto whom I write; send Thine angels to guard them, and deliver them from all evil; and when they turn their faces toward Zion, and bow down before Thee and pray, may their sins never come up before Thy face, neither have place in the book of Thy remembrance; and may they depart from all their iniquities. Provide food for them as Thou doest for the ravens; provide clothing to cover their nakedness, and houses that they may dwell therein; give unto them friends in abundance, and let their names be recorded in the Lamb's book of life, eternally before Thy face. Amen" (*History of the Church of Jesus Christ of Latter-day Saints,* 7 vols. [1932–1951], 1:456).

Now, after such a pleading, listen to the faith in this account, written by the Prophet Joseph on March 1, 1842, after the sorrows of Missouri and in the promise of Nauvoo. See if disappointment has dimmed faith.

"We next settled in Caldwell and Daviess counties, where we made large and extensive settlements, thinking to free ourselves from the power of oppression, by settling in new counties, with very few inhabitants in them; but here we were not allowed to live in peace, but in 1838 we were again attacked by mobs, an exterminating order was issued by Governor Boggs, and under the sanction of law, an organized banditti ranged through the country, robbed us of our cattle, sheep, hogs, &c., many of our people were murdered in cold blood, the chastity of our women was violated, and we were forced to sign away our property at the point of the sword; and after enduring every indignity that could be heaped upon us by an inhuman, ungodly band of marauders, from twelve to fifteen thousand souls, men, women, and children were driven from their own firesides, and from lands to which they had warrantee deeds, houseless, friendless, and homeless (in the depths of winter) to wander as exiles on the earth, or to seek an asylum in a more genial clime, and among a less barbarous people. Many sickened and died in consequence of the cold and hardships they had to endure; many wives were left widows, and children, orphans, and destitute."

The statement then goes on to say:

"In the situation before alluded to, we arrived in the state of Illinois in 1839, where we found a hospitable people and a friendly home: a people who were willing to be governed by the principles of law and humanity. We have commenced to build a city called 'Nauvoo,' in Hancock county. We number from six to eight thousand here, besides vast numbers in the county around, and in almost every county of the state. We have a city charter granted us, and charter for a Legion, the troops of which now number 1,500. We have also a charter for a University, for an Agricultural and Manufacturing Society, have our own laws and administrators, and possess all the privileges that other free and enlightened citizens enjoy.

"Persecution has not stopped the progress of truth, but has only added fuel to the flame, it has spread with increasing rapidity. Proud of the cause which they have espoused, and conscious of our innocence, and of the truth of their system, amidst calumny and reproach, have the Elders of this Church gone forth, and planted the Gospel in almost every state in the Union; it has penetrated our cities, it has spread over our villages, and has caused thousands of our intelligent, noble, and patriotic citizens to obey its divine mandates, and be governed by its sacred truths. It has also spread into England, Ireland, Scotland, and Wales, where, in the year 1840, a few of our missionaries were sent, and over five thousand joined the Standard of Truth; there are numbers now joining in every land.

"Our missionaries are going forth to different nations, and in Germany, Palestine, New Holland, Australia, the East Indies, and other places, the Standard of Truth has been erected; no unhallowed hand can stop the work from progressing; persecutions may rage, mobs may combine, armies may assemble, calumny may defame, but the truth of God will go forth boldly, nobly, and independent, till it has penetrated every continent, visited every clime, swept every country, and sounded in every ear, till the purposes of God shall be accomplished, and the Great Jehovah shall say the work is done" ("The Wentworth Letter," in *History of the Church,* 4:539–40).

The Prophet and the faithful Saints expected trials. They knew the Lord would deliver them. They believed what Nephi taught:

"But behold, I, Nephi, will show unto you that the tender mercies of the Lord are over all those whom he hath chosen, because of their faith, to make them mighty even unto the power of deliverance" (1 Nephi 1:20).

And they knew they would need such deliverance time and time again, as opposition would rise. They knew that the times of peace would be temporary, and so made of them times of gratitude and of boldness to go forward with the work.

As the leaders grew in faith through the cycles of opposition and deliverance followed by more opposition, so did the people. One was my great-grandmother, Mary Bommeli, a little black-eyed, teenage convert from Switzerland when she crossed the plains. I recently stood in the area of her childhood. I had always pictured it as on the side of an alp, but I was wrong. It is in the green rolling hills of northern Switzerland, with rich farmland and productive vineyards. I wish we had been able to find the house where the missionaries taught her and her family and where they all came to know that the gospel of Jesus Christ and the kingdom of God had been restored and where they chose to give their lives to the kingdom—the older boys to go on missions and the rest to gather to America to build Zion. They left a beautiful place of safety for the unknown.

Mary chose to let the others go first without her. She knew she could make the money for passage with her weaving but that the others could not. She chose to let them go on missions and to America using all the money they could get from selling all they owned. She went alone from city to city weaving cloth for women, trusting in God. She also got herself arrested for preaching the gospel where it was illegal in Germany because she could not contain the good news within her.

She got to America, joined a pioneer company, and walked across the plains. She described that crossing on foot as one of the happiest times of her life. On that walk she met a returning missionary, Henry Eyring. They went in front of the wagon train to be clear of the dust. They described that trek not as a trial but as a time of joy as they told each

The Prophet and the faithful Saints expected trials. They knew the Lord would deliver them. And they knew they would need such deliverance time and time again, as opposition would rise. They knew that the times of peace would be temporary, and so made of them times of gratitude and of boldness to go forward with the work.

other what a remarkable chance was theirs to have been found by the servants of God and to be allowed to help build the kingdom of God in the last days. They fell in love. For them, that passage was not a trial but a time of refreshing, of refuge. They chose to see in it a respite, he from his five-year mission and she from working her way alone from Switzerland. It was their youthful faith that made it a romantic stroll.

For Mary and for Henry, the trials began in the promised land. After their marriage, only Mary's weaving kept them from starvation. Henry was university-trained in Germany but ignorant of the skills needed to pioneer in the wilderness. They built a small home. Neither of them knew how to make adobe bricks. When the rains came, the roof leaked and then a wall collapsed. It fell on Mary, who was pregnant with their first child. Only the remarkable fact that her loom protected her from the falling bricks saved her from greater harm. But the child she was carrying was injured. He was born with physical handicaps from which he was delivered only by death.

With ceaseless labor and prayers they began to rise from poverty, in Davis County and in Salt Lake City. But that time of peace was cut short. President Brigham Young suggested that they move to St. George. They went to the unknown again, built homes, planted gardens, and served in the kingdom. Henry became the mayor of St. George for a time, a counselor in the stake presidency, and manager of the cooperative store. They helped build the St. George Temple, and Mary found joy in officiating there for twelve years. She wrote of that service as if she had felt the peace the Lord promised when He commanded that a temple be built long before.

This is the promise from the book of Haggai in the Old Testament: "The glory of this latter house shall be greater than of the former, saith the Lord of hosts: and in this place will I give peace, saith the Lord of hosts" (Haggai 2:9).

But Mary heard what she considered a call from an Apostle to move on from that time of peace. It was suggested that they join in the establishment of the Mormon colonies in northern Mexico. They went believing that the Lord would sustain them in His service.

They saw more safety going forward to unknown service in the kingdom than in staying with the known and the comfortable. They left what had become for them a Zion to help the Lord build another—not out of blind obedience, since they were invited and not called, but in faith that the wisest course for them was to go where they might best build the kingdom.

In Mexico the pattern of deliverance repeated itself for them. In time they were blessed with homes and gardens. Henry went away on a mission to the south in Mexico, as he had previously done from Utah to Germany, and he built up the cooperative store in Colonia Juarez as he had in St. George. Mary again gave tireless service in Relief Society. Their work and their faith again brought a taste of the peace that will be in the city of Zion. And then Henry died. The Mexican Revolution came. Mary and her family walked away from all they had built as they made their exodus to the United States. She died a widow, a refugee from that idyllic time in Mexico, yet full of faith in the destiny of the kingdom of God and in its head, Jesus Christ, as her deliverer.

Mary's story is worth telling not because it is exceptional but because it isn't. The growth in her faith seemed as constant in times of deliverance as it was in times of trial. That seems to have been true for each pioneer whose story I read. It seems to me that was true because their faith was based on an understanding of why God allows us to pass into such close places and how He delivers us. The "how" springs from the "why." The why is that our loving Heavenly Father and His Son, Jesus Christ, wish for us to be sanctified that we may have eternal life with them. That requires our being cleansed through faith in Jesus Christ, repenting because of that faith, and proving ourselves faithful to the covenants they offer us only through their mortal servants in the kingdom of God. Knowing their loving purpose makes it easier to understand both why they allow trials and how they deliver us.

They could make all the rough places smooth in building the kingdom and in our lives. They allow trials to come even when we are faithful because they love us. There are some scriptures that now seem clearer to me after reading those pioneer journals.

This one is from Doctrine and Covenants 105:19:

"I have heard their prayers, and will accept their offering; and it is expedient in me that they should be brought thus far for a trial of their faith."

Our loving Heavenly Father and His Son, Jesus Christ, wish for us to be sanctified that we may have eternal life with them. That requires our being cleansed through faith in Jesus Christ, repenting because of that faith, and proving ourselves faithful to the covenants they offer us only through their mortal servants in the kingdom of God.

Here is another we have heard often, from Ether 12:6:

"And now, I, Moroni, would speak somewhat concerning these things; I would show unto the world that faith is things which are hoped for and not seen; wherefore, dispute not because ye see not, for ye receive no witness until after the trial of your faith."

But for me, the greatest comfort comes from this one in Doctrine and Covenants 95:1:

"Verily, thus saith the Lord unto you whom I love, and whom I love I also chasten that their sins may be forgiven, for with the chastisement I prepare a way for their deliverance in all things out of temptation, and I have loved you."

I have come to understand that to try our faith is not simply to test it but to strengthen it, that the witness which comes after the testing strengthens that faith, and that God's preparation includes in the plan for deliverance the timing that will best strengthen our faith.

It is clear that the quickest deliverance does not always go to those with the most faith. A remarkable example of immediate deliverance is the preservation of the children of Israel not when they were full of faith but when they murmured. You remember their complaint and the Lord's answer through Moses:

God's preparation includes in the plan for deliverance the timing that will best strengthen our faith.

"Is not this the word that we did tell thee in Egypt, saying, Let us alone, that we may serve the Egyptians? For it had been better for us to serve the Egyptians, than that we should die in the wilderness.

"And Moses said unto the people, Fear ye not, stand still, and see the salvation of the Lord, which he will shew to you to day: for the Egyptians whom ye have seen to day, ye shall see them again no more for ever" (Exodus 14:12–13).

A loving father may have given speedy deliverance to help their wavering faith, but those with greater faith may gain more from delay. At least that seems to be the lot of some of the best and most faithful people. It is for such faithful Saints that the Lord may be giving reassurance in the words of Doctrine and Covenants 58:3–4:

"Ye cannot behold with your natural eyes, for the present time, the design of your God concerning those things which shall come hereafter, and the glory which shall follow after much tribulation.

"For after much tribulation come the blessings. Wherefore the day cometh that ye shall be crowned with much glory; the hour is not yet, but is nigh at hand."

The Lord's "nigh at hand" is often not as nigh as we would choose. But He sometimes honors the most faithful by offering the chance to share His view of time. And we stand in awe of those who patiently bow to the Lord's longer view, in the process becoming more like Him, beginning to see as He sees.

> *The Lord's "nigh at hand" is often not as nigh as we would choose. But He sometimes honors the most faithful by offering the chance to share His view of time.*

Some of our trials do not end in this life. For that, our Lord promises us strength to endure this way:

"And now, O my son Helaman, behold, thou art in thy youth, and therefore, I beseech of thee that thou wilt hear my words and learn of me; for I do know that whosoever shall put their trust in God shall be supported in their trials, and their troubles, and their afflictions, and shall be lifted up at the last day" (Alma 36:3).

Of all the tests we face, none hurts more than the death of a loved one or the misery of sin. Through the resurrection of Jesus Christ all are delivered from death, and all will rise in the Resurrection, regardless of their transgressions. And by the Atonement of Jesus Christ, all may gain peace in this life washed clean from the sorrows of sin and have hope of a glorious resurrection with the just.

I listened to a man describe what it meant to his family to be built on the foundation of Jesus Christ. For them it was to know that their son would rise in the Resurrection; there he could finish the training of his infant son from whom he had been parted by death. Through their faith in the Savior, the family was delivered from sorrow and lifted to a place of peace. Gratitude for such

deliverance appears often in the histories of pioneers, partly because death struck so often so early.

We find less mention of the deliverance from sin, since that is
so private a matter. But it was there as surely as it is in our lives.
Each of us has in some degree felt the deliverance described in the
history of Alma the Younger. You remember his words, which glad-
den us every time we hear them and bring back floods of gratitude
for our own deliverance:

"And now, behold, when I thought this, I could remember my
pains no more; yea, I was harrowed up by the memory of my sins
no more.

"And oh, what joy, and what marvelous light I did behold; yea,
my soul was filled with joy as exceeding as was my pain!

"Yea, I say unto you, my son, that there could be nothing so
exquisite and so bitter as were my pains. Yea, and again I say unto
you, my son, that on the other hand, there can be nothing so exquisite and sweet as was my joy.

"Yea, methought I saw, even as our father Lehi saw, God sitting
upon his throne, surrounded with numberless concourses of angels, in the attitude of singing and praising their God; yea, and my
soul did long to be there" (Alma 36:19–22).

The peace of forgiveness and of hope in the Resurrection can
come wherever we are. The peace that passeth understanding does
not depend on a geographic place. The place of refuge is finally
in our hearts. The Lord had at least two meanings when He said,
"Therefore, verily, thus saith the Lord, let Zion rejoice, for this is
Zion—the pure in heart" (Doctrine and Covenants 97:21). Zion
is where the pure in heart are gathered; that gathering creates a
Zion. But in one person whose heart is cleansed by the Atonement
and filled with the hope of eternal life there is a place of peace and
refuge, too.

With that feeling of peace comes a desire to serve. That is why those who have felt the blessings of baptism and confirmation feel impelled to share the gospel with others. That's why Mary Bommeli went to jail. Whatever our circumstances, we can remember the Savior and that we are blessed to be in His kingdom, and we can have in our hearts the question "How would the Master have me serve him?" If we ask that in faith, with determination to follow the promptings that come from the Holy Spirit, those promptings will come. We will discover plans to help build the kingdom. We will be refreshed in our hearts and sure that what our pioneers believed was true: the kingdom of God has been restored and we are blessed as the few among our Father's myriad children to build it for the Master for the last time.

The peace that passeth understanding does not depend on a geographic place. The place of refuge is finally in our hearts.

The Power of Deliverance

I wish to bear witness of God's power of deliverance. At some point in our lives we will all need that power. Every person living is in the midst of a test. We have been granted by God the precious gift of life in a world created as a proving ground and a preparatory school. The tests we will face, their severity, their timing, and their duration will be unique for each of us. But two things will be the same for all of us. They are part of the design for mortal life.

First, the tests at times will stretch us enough for us to feel the need for help beyond our own. And, second, God in His kindness and wisdom has made the power of deliverance available to us.

Now you might well ask, "Since Heavenly Father loves us, why does His plan of happiness include trials that could overwhelm us?" It is because His purpose is to offer us eternal life. He wants to give us a happiness that is only possible as we live as families forever in glory with Him. And trials are necessary for us to be shaped and made fit

> *Trials are necessary for us to be shaped and made fit to receive that happiness that comes as we qualify for the greatest of all the gifts of God.*

to receive that happiness that comes as we qualify for the greatest of all the gifts of God.

There are many different tests, but here I will speak of only three. You may be in one of these tests now. For each, the power of deliverance is available—not to escape the test but to endure it well.

First: We can feel overcome with pain and sorrow at the death of a loved one.

Second: Each of us will struggle against fierce opposition— some of which comes from dealing with our physical needs and some from enemies.

Third: Each of us who live past the age of accountability will feel the need to escape from the effects of sin.

Each of these tests can provide the opportunity for us to see that we need the power of God to help us pass them well.

Some of you may feel the pressures of those tests now, but all of us will face them. It helps to know that they do not come from random chance or from a cruel God. And knowing what a wonderful reward lies ahead helps us to endure the tests well. The Prophet Joseph Smith needed and got that assurance when he was feeling deserted and nearly overwhelmed by persecution and contention among those he led and loved:

"My son, peace be unto thy soul; thine adversity and thine afflictions shall be but a small moment;

"And then, if thou endure it well, God shall exalt thee on high" (Doctrine and Covenants 121:7–8).

The Lord told Joseph that his trials would be for a small moment. That was true for him, and it will be for us as we compare the duration of any earthly trial with the endlessness of eternity. And the reward for passing the tests well is to become worthy of eternal life. That assurance will help us when enemies defame us or doctors deliver a grim prognosis.

That brings us to the first category of trials we will consider: the tragedy that death can bring. Life ends early for some and eventually for us all. Each of us will be tested by facing the death of someone we love. Just the other day I met a man I had not seen since his wife died. It was a chance meeting in a pleasant social holiday situation. He was smiling as he approached me. Remembering his wife's death, I phrased the common greeting very carefully: "How are you doing?"

The smile vanished, his eyes became moist, and he said

Through His experience the Savior came to know all our griefs. He could have known them by the inspiration of the Spirit. But He chose instead to know by experiencing them for Himself.

quietly, with great earnestness, "I'm doing fine. But it's very hard."

It is very hard, as most of you have learned and all of us will sometime know. The hardest part of that test is to know what to do with the sorrow, the loneliness, and the loss that can feel as if a part of us has been lost. Grief can persist like a chronic ache. And for some there may be feelings of anger or injustice.

The Savior's Atonement and Resurrection give Him the power to deliver us in such a trial. Through His experience He came to know all our griefs. He could have known them by the inspiration of the Spirit. But He chose instead to know by experiencing them for Himself. This is the account:

"And behold, he shall be born of Mary, at Jerusalem which is the land of our forefathers, she being a virgin, a precious and chosen vessel, who shall be overshadowed and conceive by the power of the Holy Ghost, and bring forth a son, yea, even the Son of God.

"And he shall go forth, suffering pains and afflictions and temptations of every kind; and this that the word might be fulfilled which saith he will take upon him the pains and the sicknesses of his people.

"And he will take upon him death, that he may loose the bands of death which bind his people; and he will take upon him their infirmities, that his bowels may be filled with mercy, according to the flesh, that he may know according to the flesh how to succor his people according to their infirmities" (Alma 7:10–12).

Good people around you will try to understand your grief at the passing of a loved one. They may feel grief themselves. The Savior not only understands and feels grief but also feels *your* personal grief that only you feel. And He knows you perfectly. He knows your heart. So He can know which of the many things you can do that will be best for you as you invite the Holy Ghost to comfort and bless you. He will know where it is best for you to start. Sometimes it will be to pray. It might be to go to comfort someone else. I know of a widow with a debilitating illness who was inspired to visit another widow. I wasn't there, but I am certain that the Lord inspired a faithful disciple to reach out to another and thus was able to succor them both.

There are many ways that the Savior can succor those who grieve, each fitted to them. But you can be sure that He can and that He will do it in the way that is best for those who grieve and for those around them. The constant when God delivers people from grief is people feeling childlike humility before God. A great example of the power of that faithful humility comes from the life of Job. You remember the account:

"Then Job arose, and rent his mantle, and shaved his head, and fell down upon the ground, and worshipped,

"And said, Naked came I out of my mother's womb, and naked shall I return thither: the Lord gave, and the Lord hath taken away; blessed be the name of the Lord.

"In all this Job sinned not, nor charged God foolishly" (Job 1:20–22).

Humility is one constant in those who are delivered from grief. The other, which Job had, is abiding faith in the power of the Savior's Resurrection. We all will be resurrected. The loved one who dies will be resurrected as the Savior was. The reunion we will have with them will not be ethereal but with bodies that need never die nor age nor become infirm.

There are many ways that the Savior can succor those who grieve, each fitted to them. But you can be sure that He can and that He will do it in the way that is best for those who grieve and for those around them.

When the Savior appeared to His apostles after the Resurrection, He not only reassured them in their grief but also all of us who might ever grieve. He reassured them and us this way:

"Peace be unto you. . . .

"Behold my hands and my feet, that it is I myself: handle me, and see; for a spirit hath not flesh and bones, as ye see me have: (Luke 24:36, 39).

The Lord can inspire us to reach out for the power of deliverance from our grief in the way best suited to us. We can invite the Holy Ghost in humble prayer. We can choose to serve others for the Lord. We can testify of the Savior, of His gospel, and of His Restoration of His Church. We can keep His commandments. All of those choices invite the Holy Ghost. It is the Holy Ghost who can comfort us in the way suited to our need. And by the inspiration of the Spirit we can have a testimony of the Resurrection and a clear view of the glorious reunion ahead. I have felt that comfort as I looked down at the gravestone of someone I knew—someone that I know I can at some future time hold in my arms. Knowing that, I was not only delivered from grief but was filled with happy anticipation.

Had that little person lived to maturity, she would have needed deliverance in another set of trials. She would have been tested to stay faithful to God through the physical and spiritual challenges that come to everyone. Even though the body is a magnificent creation, keeping it functioning is a challenge that tests us all. For too many in the world it is hard to find enough food and clean water to get through the next day. Everyone must struggle through illness and the effects of aging.

Beyond the challenges of the body that come from within, we face the opposition of enemies from without. There is anger and hatred in the world around us, and some of it will at times be directed at us. As the Prophet Joseph learned, the opposition grew as he became more valuable to the Lord's purposes.

The power of deliverance from these trials is in place. It works in the same way as the deliverance from the trial that comes in facing the death of a loved one. Just as that deliverance is not always to have spared the life of a loved one, the deliverance from other trials may not be to remove them. It may not be to have perfect health or to have enemies vanish or ignore us. He may not give relief until we develop faith to make choices that will bring the power of the Atonement to work in our lives. He does not require that out of indifference but out of love for us. Here is His warning:

"For behold, the Lord hath said: I will not succor my people in the day of their transgression; but I will hedge up their ways that they prosper not; and their doings shall be as a stumbling block before them" (Mosiah 7:29).

There is a guide for receiving the Lord's power of deliverance from opposition in life. It was given to Thomas B. Marsh, then the president of the Quorum of the Twelve Apostles. He was in difficult trials, and the Lord knew he would face more. Here was the counsel to him that I take for myself and offer you: "Be thou humble; and the Lord thy God shall lead thee by the hand, and give thee answer to thy prayers" (Doctrine and Covenants 112:10).

The way to deliverance always requires humility in order for the Lord to be able to lead us by the hand where He wants to take us through our troubles and on to sanctification.

The Lord always wants to lead us to deliverance through our becoming more righteous. That requires repentance. And that takes humility. So the way to deliverance always requires humility in order for the Lord to be able to lead us by the hand where He wants to take us through our troubles and on to sanctification.

We might make the mistake of assuming that illness, persecution, and poverty will be humbling enough. They don't always produce by themselves the kind and degree of humility we will need to be rescued. Trials can produce resentment or discouragement. The humility you and I need to get the Lord to lead us by the hand comes from faith. It comes from faith that God really lives, that He loves us, and that what He wants—hard as it may be—will always be best for us.

The Savior showed us that humility. You have read of how He prayed in the garden while He was suffering a trial on our behalf beyond our ability to comprehend or to endure, or even for me to describe. You remember His prayer: "Father, if thou be willing, remove this cup from me: nevertheless not my will, but thine, be done" (Luke 22:42).

He knew and trusted His Heavenly Father, the great Elohim. He knew that His Father was all powerful and infinitely kind. The Beloved Son asked for the power of deliverance to help Him in humble words like those of a little child.

The Father did not deliver the Son by removing the trial. For our sakes He did not do that, and He allowed the Savior to finish the mission He came to perform. Yet we can forever take courage and comfort from knowing of the help that the Father did provide:

"And there appeared an angel unto him from heaven, strengthening him.

"And being in an agony he prayed more earnestly: and his sweat was as it were great drops of blood falling down to the ground.

"And when he rose up from prayer, and was come to his disciples, he found them sleeping for sorrow,

"And said unto them, Why sleep ye? rise and pray, lest ye enter into temptation" (Luke 22:43–46).

The Savior prayed for deliverance. What He was given was not an escape from the trial but comfort enough to pass through it gloriously.

His command to His disciples, who were themselves being tested, is a guide for us. We can determine to follow it. We can determine to rise up and pray in great faith and humility. And we can follow the command added in the book of Mark: "Rise up, let us go" (Mark 14:42).

From this you have counsel for passing the physical and spiritual tests of life. You will need God's help after you have done all you can for yourself. So rise up and go, but get His help as early as you can, not waiting for the crisis to ask for deliverance.

In life you will face stumbling blocks and opposition. You can and must go forward with confidence. If you start determined to qualify for God's power of deliverance in all the trials of mortality, you will succeed. You will be strengthened. You will be guided around and through barriers. Help and comfort will come. Your faith in Heavenly Father and the Savior will be increased. You will be strengthened to resist evil. And you will feel the gospel of Jesus Christ working in your life.

> *In life you will face stumbling blocks and opposition. You can and must go forward with confidence. If you start determined to qualify for God's power of deliverance in all the trials of mortality, you will succeed.*

And that brings us to the third trial. All of us will at times struggle to feel free from the effects of sin. Only the Savior had the power to resist every temptation and never sin. So the most important and most difficult trial for us all is to become clean and to know that we are. All of us yearn at times for the confidence that we will see the Lord's face—as we will, in the final judgment—and see it with joy and pleasure.

As we understand about trials and what it takes to get the powers of deliverance, you and I can hope for happiness in that day of judgment that will come for all of us. What it takes to qualify for the powers of deliverance in the trials of life also can qualify us for the assurance we need that we will have passed the ultimate test of mortality.

We have seen that deliverance always requires humility before God. It takes submission to His will. It takes prayer and the willingness to obey. It takes serving others out of love for them and for the Savior. And it always requires and invites the Holy Ghost.

As you are delivered in trials, the Holy Ghost comes to you. Many of you have felt the result of frequent contact with the Holy Ghost. It may have been in your missionary service, where you needed deliverance many times. The Holy Ghost came to comfort and to guide you. As that recurred again and again, you may have noticed a change in yourself. The temptations that once troubled you seemed to fade. People who once seemed difficult began to appear more lovable. You began to see almost unreasonable potential in very humble people. You came to care more about their happiness than about your own.

If that change in you came, it was more likely gradual than sudden. Yet it was what the scriptures call the "mighty change" (Mosiah 5:2; Alma 5:12–14). And it is the evidence you and I need to have hope and assurance as we look forward to the great and final test, the Final Judgment that comes after this life. Your experience in enduring well in the trials of life by drawing on God's power of deliverance can bring you the assurance you need to find peace in this life and confidence for the next.

In the Strength
of the Lord

W hen I was a young man, I served as counselor to a wise district president in the Church. He tried to teach me. One of the things I remember wondering about was this advice he gave: "When you meet someone, treat them as if they were in serious trouble, and you will be right more than half the time."

I thought then that he was pessimistic. Now, more than forty years later, I can see how well he understood the world and life. As time passes, the world grows more challenging, and our physical capacities slowly diminish with age. It is clear that we will need more than human strength. The Psalmist was right: "But the salvation of the righteous is of the Lord: he is their strength in the time of trouble" (Psalm 37:39).

The restored gospel of Jesus Christ gives us help in knowing how to qualify for the strength of the Lord as we deal with adversity. It tells us why we face tests in life. And, even more importantly, it tells us how to get protection and help from the Lord.

We have trials to face because our Heavenly Father loves us. His purpose is to help us qualify for the blessing of living with Him and His Son, Jesus Christ, forever in glory and in families. To qualify for that gift we had to receive a mortal body. With that mortality we understood that we would be tested by temptations and by difficulties.

The restored gospel not only teaches us why we must be tested, but it makes clear to us what the test is. The Prophet Joseph Smith gave us an explanation. By revelation, he was able to record words spoken at the Creation of the world. They are about us, those of the spirit children of our Heavenly Father who would come into mortality. Here are the words:

"And we will prove them herewith, to see if they will do all things whatsoever the Lord their God shall command them" (Abraham 3:25).

That explanation helps us understand why we face trials in life. They give us the opportunity to prove ourselves faithful to God. So many things beat upon us in a lifetime that simply enduring may seem almost beyond us. That's what the words in the scripture "Ye must . . . endure to the end" (2 Nephi 31:20) seemed to mean to me when I first read them. It sounded grim, like sitting still and holding on to the arms of the chair while someone pulled out my tooth.

It can surely seem that way to a family depending on crops when there is no rain. They may wonder, "How long can we hold on?" It can seem that way to a youth faced with resisting the rising flood of filth and temptation. It can seem that way to a young man struggling to get the training he needs for a job to support a wife and family. It can seem that way to a person who can't find a job or who has lost job after job as businesses close their doors. It can seem that way to a person faced with the erosion of health and physical strength which may come early or late in life for them or for those they love.

But the test a loving God has set before us is not to see if we can endure difficulty. It is to see if we can endure it well. We pass the test by showing that we remembered Him and the commandments He gave us. And to endure well is to keep those commandments whatever the opposition, whatever the temptation, and whatever the tumult around us. We have that clear understanding because the restored gospel makes the plan of happiness so plain.

That clarity lets us see what help we need. We need strength beyond ourselves to keep the commandments in whatever circumstance life brings to us. For some it may be poverty, but for others it may be prosperity. It may be the ravages of age or the exuberance of youth. The combination of trials and their duration are as varied as are the children of our Heavenly Father. No two are alike. But what is being tested is the same, at all times in our lives and for every person: will we do whatsoever the Lord our God will command us?

Knowing why we are tested and what the test is tells us how to get help. We have to go to God. He gives us the commandments. And we will need more than our own strength to keep them.

The test a loving God has set before us is not to see if we can endure difficulty. It is to see if we can endure it well. We pass the test by showing that we remembered Him and the commandments He gave us.

Again, the restored gospel makes plain the simple things we need to do. And it gives us confidence that the help we need will come if we do those things early and persistently, long before the moment of crisis.

The first, the middle, and the last thing to do is to pray. The Savior told us how. One of the clearest instructions is in 3 Nephi:

"Behold, verily, verily, I say unto you, ye must watch and pray always lest ye enter into temptation; for Satan desireth to have you, that he may sift you as wheat.

"Therefore ye must always pray unto the Father in my name;

"And whatsoever ye shall ask the Father in my name, which is right, believing that ye shall receive, behold it shall be given unto you.

"Pray in your families unto the Father, always in my name, that your wives and your children may be blessed" (3 Nephi 18:18–21). So, we must pray always.

Another simple thing to do, which allows God to give us strength, is to feast on the word of God: read and ponder the standard works of the Church and the words of living prophets. There is a promise of help from God that comes with that daily practice. Faithful study of scriptures brings the Holy Ghost to us. The promise is given in the Book of Mormon, but it applies as well to all the words of God that He has given and will give us through His prophets.

"Behold, I would exhort you that when ye shall read these things, if it be wisdom in God that ye should read them, that ye would remember how merciful the Lord hath been unto the children of men, from the creation of Adam even down until the time that ye shall receive these things, and ponder it in your hearts.

"And when ye shall receive these things, I would exhort you that ye would ask God, the Eternal Father, in the name of Christ, if these things are not true; and if ye shall ask with a sincere heart, with real intent, having faith in Christ, he will manifest the truth of it unto you, by the power of the Holy Ghost.

"And by the power of the Holy Ghost ye may know the truth of all things" (Moroni 10:3–5).

We should claim the promise not only once nor only for the Book of Mormon. The promise is sure. The power of the Holy Ghost is real. It will come, again and again. And one overriding truth it will always testify to is that Jesus is the Christ.

That testimony will draw us to the Savior and to accepting the help He offers to all who are being tested in the crucible of mortality. More than once He has said that He would gather us to Him as a hen would gather her chickens under her wings. He says that we must choose to come to Him in meekness and with enough faith in Him to repent "with full purpose of heart" (3 Nephi 10:6).

One way to do that is to gather with the Saints in His Church. Go to your meetings, even when it seems hard. If you are determined, He will help you find the strength to do it.

A member wrote to me from England. When her bishop asked if she would accept a call to teach early-morning seminary, he told her she'd better pray about it before she accepted. She did. She accepted. When she met the parents for the first time the bishop stood beside her. She announced that she felt the program should go to five days a week. Some parents looked doubtful. One person said, "They won't come. They'll vote with their feet."

Well, the doubt was half right. The students did vote with their feet. But their attendance in those cold and dark morning hours is now above 90 percent. That teacher and her bishop believed that if the students would start to come they would be strengthened

> *The power of the Holy Ghost is real. It will come, again and again. And one overriding truth it will always testify to is that Jesus is the Christ. That testimony will draw us to the Savior and to accepting the help He offers to all who are being tested in the crucible of mortality.*

by power more than their own. It came. That power will protect them when they go to places where they will be the only Latter-day Saints. They will not be alone nor without strength, because they accepted the invitation to gather with the Saints when it was not easy.

That strength is given to those who are older as well as the young. I know a widow more than ninety years of age. She is in a wheelchair. She prays as you do, pleading for help to solve problems beyond her human power to resolve. The answer is a feeling in her heart. It draws her to keep a commandment: "And behold, ye shall meet together oft" (3 Nephi 18:22). So she finds a way to get to her meetings. People who attend there have told me, "We are so glad to see her. She brings such a spirit with her."

She partakes of the sacrament, and she renews a covenant. She remembers the Savior, and she tries to keep His commandments. And so she takes His Spirit with her, always. Her problems may not be resolved. Most of them come from the choices of others, and even the Heavenly Father who hears her prayers and loves her cannot force others to choose the right. But He can send her to the safety of the Savior and the promise of His Spirit to be with her. And so I am sure that she will, in the strength of the Lord, pass the test she faces, because she keeps the commandment to gather often with the Saints. That is both the evidence that she is enduring well and the source of her strength for what lies ahead.

There is another simple thing to do. The Lord's Church has been restored, and so any call to serve in it is a call to serve Him. That bishop in England was so wise. He asked the woman to pray about her call to serve. He knew what answer she would receive. It would be an invitation from the Father and His Beloved Son. He knew what she has learned by responding to the call from the Master. In His service the Holy Ghost comes as a companion to those who try to do the best they can. She must have felt that as she stood before the parents and when she saw the students vote with their feet. What looked hard, almost impossible under her own power, became a joy in the strength of the Lord.

When she reads and ponders over the scriptures and prays to prepare for those classes, she knows that the Savior has asked the Father to send her the Holy Ghost, just as He promised His disciples He would at the Last Supper, when He knew what trials they would face and that He must leave them. He did not leave them comfortless. He promised them the Holy Ghost, and He promises it to us in His service. So, whenever the invitation to serve comes, take it. It brings with it help to pass tests far beyond those of that call.

> *In the Master's service, you will come to know and love Him. You will, if you persevere in prayer and faithful service, begin to sense that the Holy Ghost has become a companion.*

Now not all have formal calls. But every disciple serves the Master by bearing testimony and being kind to people around them. All have promised in the waters of baptism to do that. And all will gain the companionship of the Spirit as they persist in keeping their commitments with God.

In the Master's service, you will come to know and love Him. You will, if you persevere in prayer and faithful service, begin to sense that the Holy Ghost has become a companion. Many of us have for a period given such service and felt that companionship. If you think back on that time, you will remember that there were changes in you. The temptation to do evil seemed to lessen. The desire to do good increased. Those who knew you best and loved you may have said, "You have become more kind, more patient. You don't seem to be the same person."

You weren't the same person because the Atonement of Jesus Christ is real. And the promise is real that we can become new, changed, and better. And we can become stronger for the tests of life. We then go in the strength of the Lord, a strength developed in His service. He goes with us. And in time we become His tested and strengthened disciples.

You will then notice a change in your prayers. They will become more fervent and more frequent. The words you speak will have a different meaning to you. By commandment we always pray to the Father in the name of Jesus Christ. But you will feel a greater confidence as you pray to the Father, knowing that you go to Him as a trusted and proven disciple of Jesus Christ. The Father will grant you greater peace and strength in this life and with it a happy anticipation of hearing the words, when the test of life is over, "Well done, thou good and faithful servant" (Matthew 25:21).

POWER TO LIVE A
CONSECRATED LIFE

OPPORTUNITIES TO
DO GOOD

Our Heavenly Father hears the prayers of His children across the earth pleading for food to eat, for clothes to cover their bodies, and for the dignity that would come from being able to provide for themselves. Those pleas have reached Him since He placed men and women on the earth.

You learn of those needs where you live and from across the world. Your heart is often stirred with feelings of sympathy. When you meet someone struggling to find employment, you feel that desire to help. You feel it when you go into the home of a widow and see that she has no food. You feel it when you see photographs of crying children sitting in the ruins of their home destroyed by an earthquake or by fire.

Because the Lord hears their cries and feels your deep compassion for them, He has from the beginning of time provided ways for His disciples to help. He has invited His children to consecrate their time, their means, and themselves to join with Him in serving others.

His way of helping has at times been called living the law of consecration. In another period His way was called the united order. In our time it is called the Church welfare program.

The names and the details of operation are changed to fit the needs and conditions of people. But always the Lord's way to help those in temporal need requires people who out of love have consecrated themselves and what they have to God and to His work.

He has invited and commanded us to participate in His work to lift up those in need. We make a covenant to do that in the waters of baptism and in the holy temples of God. We renew the covenant on Sundays when we partake of the sacrament.

There is a hymn about the Lord's invitation to this work that I have sung since I was a little boy. In my childhood I paid more attention to the happy tune than to the power of the words. I pray that you will feel the lyrics in your heart:

> *Have I done any good in the world today?*
> *Have I helped anyone in need?*
> *Have I cheered up the sad and made someone feel glad?*
> *If not, I have failed indeed.*
> *Has anyone's burden been lighter today*
> *Because I was willing to share?*
> *Have the sick and the weary been helped on their way?*
> *When they needed my help was I there?*
> *Then wake up and do something more*
> *Than dream of your mansion above.*
> *Doing good is a pleasure, a joy beyond measure,*
> *A blessing of duty and love.*
> (Will L. Thompson, "Have I Done Any Good?"
>   *Hymns*, no. 223)

The Lord regularly sends wake-up calls to all of us. Sometimes it may be a sudden feeling of sympathy for someone in need. A father may have felt it when he saw a child fall and scrape a knee. A mother may have felt it when she heard the frightened cry of her child in the night. A son or a daughter may have felt sympathy for someone who seemed sad or afraid at school.

All of us have been touched with feelings of sympathy for others we don't even know. For instance, as you heard reports of the waves rushing across the Pacific after the earthquake in Japan, you felt concern for those who might be hurt.

Feelings of sympathy came to thousands of you who learned of the flooding in Queensland, Australia. The news reports were mainly estimates of numbers of those in need. But many of you felt the pain of the people. The wake-up call was answered by 1,500 or more Church member volunteers in Australia who came to help and to comfort.

The Lord regularly sends wake-up calls to all of us. Sometimes it may be a sudden feeling of sympathy for someone in need.

They turned their feelings of sympathy into a decision to act on their covenants. I have seen the blessings that come to the person in need who receives help and to the person who seizes the opportunity to give it.

Wise parents see in every need of others a way to bring blessings into the lives of their sons and daughters. Three children recently carried containers holding a delicious dinner to our front door. Their parents knew that we needed help, and they included their children in the opportunity to serve us.

The parents blessed our family by their generous service. By their choice to let their children participate in the giving, they extended blessings to their future grandchildren. The smiles of the children as they left our home made me confident that will happen. They will tell their children of the joy they felt giving kindly service for the Lord. I remember that feeling of quiet satisfaction from childhood as I pulled weeds for a neighbor at my father's invitation. Whenever I am invited to be a giver, I remember and believe the lyrics "Sweet is the work, my God, my King" (Isaac Watts, "Sweet Is the Work," *Hymns,* no. 147).

I know those lyrics were written to describe the joy that comes from worshipping the Lord on the Sabbath. But those children with the food at our door were feeling on a weekday the joy of doing the Lord's work. And their parents saw the opportunity to do good and spread joy over generations.

The Lord's way of caring for the needy provides another opportunity for parents to bless their children. I saw it in a chapel one Sunday. A small child handed the bishop his family's donation envelope as he entered the chapel before the sacrament meeting.

I knew the family and the boy. The family had just learned of someone in the ward in need. The boy's father had said something like this to the child as he placed a more generous fast offering than usual in the envelope: "We fasted today and prayed for those in need. Please give this envelope to the bishop for us. I know that he will give it to help those with greater needs than ours."

Instead of any hunger pangs on that Sunday, the boy will remember the day with a warm glow. I could tell from his smile and the way he held the envelope so tightly that he felt the great trust of his father to carry the family offering for the poor. He will remember that day when he is a deacon and perhaps forever.

I saw that same happiness in the faces of people who helped for the Lord in Idaho years ago. The Teton Dam burst on Saturday, June 5, 1976. Eleven people were killed. Thousands had to leave their homes in a few hours. Some homes were washed away. And hundreds of dwellings could be made habitable only through effort and means far beyond that of the owners.

Those who heard of the tragedy felt sympathy, and some felt the call to do good. Neighbors, bishops, Relief Society presidents, quorum leaders, home teachers, and visiting teachers left homes and jobs to clean out the flooded houses of others.

One couple returned to Rexburg from a vacation just after the flood. They didn't go to see their own house. Instead, they found their bishop to ask where they could help. He directed them to a family in need.

After a few days they went to check on their home. It was gone, swept away in the flood. They simply walked back to the bishop and asked, "Now what would you like us to do?"

Wherever you live, you have seen that miracle of sympathy turned to unselfish action. It may not have been in the wake of a great natural disaster. I have seen it in a priesthood quorum where a brother rises to describe the needs of a man or a woman who seeks an opportunity to work to support himself or herself and his or her family. I could feel sympathy in the room, but some suggested names of people who might employ the person who needed work.

What happened in that priesthood quorum and what happened in the flooded houses in Idaho is a manifestation of the Lord's way to help those in great need become self-reliant. We feel compassion, and we know how to act in the Lord's way to help.

The Church welfare program was started more than seventy-five years ago to meet the needs of those who lost employment, farms, and even homes in the wake of what became known as the Great Depression.

Great temporal needs of the children of Heavenly Father have come again in our time as they have and as they will in all times. The principles at the foundation of the Church welfare program are not for only one time or one place. They are for all times and all places.

Those principles are spiritual and eternal. For that reason, understanding them and putting them down into our hearts will make it possible for us to see and take opportunities to help whenever and wherever the Lord invites us.

> *The principles at the foundation of the Church welfare program are not for only one time or one place. They are spiritual and eternal. For that reason, understanding them and putting them down into our hearts will make it possible for us to see and take opportunities to help whenever and wherever the Lord invites us.*

Here are some principles that guided me when I wanted to help in the Lord's way and when I have been helped by others.

First, all people are happier and feel more self-respect when they can provide for themselves and their family and then reach out to take care of others. I have been grateful for those who helped me meet my needs. I have been even more grateful over the years for those who helped me become self-reliant. And then I have been most grateful for those who showed me how to use some of my surplus to help others.

I have learned that the way to have a surplus is to spend less than I earn. With that surplus I have been able to learn that it really is better to give than to receive. That is partly because when we give help in the Lord's way, He blesses us.

President Marion G. Romney said of welfare work, "You

cannot give yourself poor in this work." And then he quoted his mission president, Melvin J. Ballard, this way: "A person cannot give a crust to the Lord without receiving a loaf in return" ("Welfare Services: The Savior's Program," *Ensign,* November 1980, 93).

I have found that to be true in my life. When I am generous to Heavenly Father's children in need, He is generous to me.

A second gospel principle that has been a guide to me in welfare work is the power and blessing of unity. When we join hands to serve people in need, the Lord unites our hearts. President J. Reuben Clark Jr. put it this way: "That giving has . . . brought . . . a feeling of common brotherhood as men of all training and occupation have worked side by side in a Welfare garden or other project" (in Conference Report, October 1943, 13).

When we join hands to serve people in need, the Lord unites our hearts.

That increased feeling of brotherhood is true for the receiver as well as the giver. To this day, a man with whom I shoveled mud side by side in his flooded Rexburg home feels a bond with me. And he feels greater personal dignity for having done all he could for himself and for his family. If we had worked alone, both of us would have lost a spiritual blessing.

That leads to the third principle of action in welfare work for me: Draw your family into the work with you so that they can learn to care for each other as they care for others. Your sons and daughters who work with you to serve others in need will be more likely to help each other when they are in need.

The fourth valuable principle of Church welfare I learned as a bishop. It came from following the scriptural command to seek out the poor. It is the duty of the bishop to find and provide help to those who still need assistance after all they and their families can do. I found that the Lord sends the Holy Ghost to make it possible to "seek, and ye shall find" (see Matthew 7:7–8) in caring for the poor as He does. But I also learned to involve the Relief Society president in the search. She may get the revelation before you do.

By the loving service you have given for the Lord, I have been the recipient of the thanks of people you have helped as I have met them across the world. You found a way to lift them higher as you helped in the Lord's way. You and humble disciples of the Savior like you have cast your bread upon the water in service, and the people you helped have tried to give me a loaf of gratitude in return.

I get that same expression of appreciation from people who have worked with you. I remember one time standing next to President Ezra Taft Benson. We had been talking about welfare service in the Lord's Church. He surprised me with his youthful vigor when he said, pumping his hand, "I love this work, and it is work!"

For the Master I extend thanks for your work to serve the children of our Heavenly Father. He knows you, and He sees your effort, diligence, and sacrifice. I pray that He will grant you the blessing of seeing the fruit of your labors in the happiness of those you have helped and with whom you have helped for the Lord.

SERVE WITH THE SPIRIT

I hold in sacred memory two priesthood bearers who had qualified for the Spirit of God to go with them on the errand to which the Lord called them. They had found the restored gospel themselves in America. They were the Lord's servants who first spoke of that gospel to two of my European ancestors.

One of those ancestors was a young girl living on a small farm in Switzerland. Another was a young man, an orphan and an immigrant to the United States from Germany, living in St. Louis, Missouri.

Both of them heard a priesthood holder testify of the restored gospel—for the girl by the fireplace of her little home in Switzerland, and for the boy it was sitting in the balcony of a rented hall in America. Both of them knew by the Spirit that the message those elders brought to them was true.

The boy and the girl chose to be baptized. The two of them met for the first time on the dusty trail years later, walking hundreds of miles to the mountains of western America. They talked as they walked. What they talked about was the miraculous blessing that in all the world, the servants of God had found them and even more miraculous, that they knew their message was true.

They fell in love and were married. And because of a testimony of the Spirit, which began as they heard the words of priesthood holders under the influence of the Holy Ghost, they were sealed for eternity by priesthood power. I am among the tens of thousands of descendants of that boy and that girl who bless the names of two priesthood holders who brought the ministrations of the Spirit of God with them as they climbed the hill in Switzerland and rose to speak in that meeting in St. Louis.

That happy story and millions more like it are repeated across the world and will be over generations. For some it will be the story of a young home teacher who said words that sparked a desire in your grandfather to come back to the Church. For some it will be the words of comfort and blessing from a patriarch that sustained your mother when tragedy nearly overwhelmed her.

There will be a common theme in all those stories. It will be the power of the priesthood in a holder whose power to serve was magnified by the Holy Ghost.

Let us do whatever is required to qualify for the Holy Ghost as our companion, and then let us go forward fearlessly so that we will be given the powers to do whatever the Lord calls us to do. That growth in power to serve may come slowly, it may come in small steps that are difficult for you to see, but it will come.

Now, we all know that confirmation into the Church gave us the gift of the Holy Ghost. But the companionship of the Holy

Let us do whatever is required to qualify for the Holy Ghost as our companion, and then let us go forward fearlessly so that we will be given the powers to do whatever the Lord calls us to do.

Ghost, the manifestations of it in our life and service, requires us to put our lives in order to qualify.

We cultivate spiritual gifts by keeping the commandments and trying to live a blameless life. That requires faith in Jesus Christ to repent and be cleansed through His Atonement. So as priesthood holders we should never miss an opportunity to participate with all our hearts in the promise offered in every sacrament meeting for members of the restored Church to "take upon them the name of [God's] Son, and always remember him and keep his commandments which he has given them; that they may always have his Spirit to be with them" (Doctrine and Covenants 20:77).

Just as we must be cleansed of sin to have the Spirit with us, we must be humble enough before God to recognize our need for it. The disciples of the resurrected Savior demonstrated that humility, as recorded in the Book of Mormon.

The Savior was preparing them for their ministry. They knelt on the ground to pray. Here is the account: "And they did pray for that which they most desired; and they desired that the Holy Ghost should be given unto them" (3 Nephi 19:9). They were baptized as you have been. And the record says that in answer to their pleading, they were filled with the Holy Ghost and with fire.

The Savior prayed aloud to thank His Father for giving the Holy Ghost to those He had chosen because of their belief in Him. And then the Savior prayed for a spiritual blessing for those they were serving. The Lord pled with His Father: "I pray thee that thou wilt give the Holy Ghost unto all them that shall believe in their words" (3 Nephi 19:21).

As the humble servants of the Savior, we should pray for the manifestations of the Holy Ghost to come to us in our service and to those we serve. Humble prayer to our Heavenly Father, in deep faith in Jesus Christ, is essential to qualify us for the companionship of the Holy Ghost.

Our humility and our faith that invite spiritual gifts are increased by our reading, studying, and pondering the scriptures. We have all heard those words. Yet we may read a few lines or pages of scripture every day and hope that will be enough.

But reading, studying, and pondering are not the same. We read words and we may get ideas. We study and we may discover patterns and connections in scripture. But when we ponder, we invite revelation by the Spirit. Pondering, to me, is the thinking and the praying I do after reading and studying in the scriptures carefully.

> *Reading, studying, and pondering are not the same. We read words and we may get ideas. We study and we may discover patterns and connections in scripture. But when we ponder, we invite revelation by the Spirit.*

For me, President Joseph F. Smith set an example of how pondering can invite light from God. It is recorded in the 138th section of the Doctrine and Covenants. He had been reading and studying many scriptures, trying to understand how the effects of the Savior's Atonement would reach those who had died never having heard His message. Here is his account of how revelation came: "As I pondered over these things which are written, the eyes of my understanding were opened, and the Spirit of the Lord rested upon me, and I saw the hosts of the dead, both small and great" (Doctrine and Covenants 138:11).

Repentance, prayer, and pondering over the scriptures are

essential parts of our qualifying for the gifts of the Spirit in our priesthood service. Further magnification of our power to serve will come as we respond with faith to go forward in our callings with the Holy Ghost to help us.

President Thomas S. Monson put it this way for us: "What does it mean to magnify [your] calling? It means to build it up in dignity . . . , to enlarge and strengthen it to let the light of heaven shine through it to the view of other men. And how does one magnify a calling? Simply by performing the service that pertains to it" ("Priesthood Power," *Ensign,* November 1999, 51).

I will suggest two services to which we are all called. In carrying them out under the influence of the Spirit, you and others will see your power to serve, strengthen, and magnify.

The first is as His agent to teach and testify to others for Him. The Lord included the youngest and the least experienced of the Aaronic Priesthood holders in that call to serve. After describing the duties of the Aaronic Priesthood holders, He said:

"But neither teachers nor deacons have authority to baptize, administer the sacrament, or lay on hands;

"They are, however, to warn, expound, exhort, and teach, and invite all to come unto Christ" (Doctrine and Covenants 20:58–59).

Somewhere in the world this week there will be a deacon asked by his quorum president to invite a member of their quorum whom he has never seen to a meeting. The thirteen-year-old president is not likely to use the words "warn, exhort, and teach," but that is what the Lord expects of the deacon assigned to go to the rescue.

To the deacon who receives the call to go to his quorum member, I will make three promises. First, as you pray for help, the Spirit will calm your fears. Second, you will be surprised that you know what to say when you get to his home and during the walk with him back to the church. What you say may seem jumbled to you. But you will feel that words were given to you at the moment you needed them. And third, you will feel the approval of the Lord, who called you through your president, whatever the outcome.

I cannot promise what success will come since every person is free to choose how he or she responds to a servant of God. But the deacon you speak to for the Lord will remember you came to him. I know of one boy, now a man still far away from Church activity, whom a deacon was sent to find, and he told his grandfather of that visit twenty years earlier. And it seemed to have no effect, and yet he even named the deacon who came. The grandfather asked me to find and thank the deacon who was called to invite, to exhort, and to teach. It had been only one day in the life of a boy, but a grandfather and the Lord remember the words the boy was inspired to speak and the boy's name.

I urge all of us, young and old, who are called to speak in a meeting in the name of the Lord to dismiss our feelings of self-doubt and inadequacy. We don't have to use soaring language or convey deep insights. Simple words of testimony will do. The Spirit will give you the words for you to speak and will carry them down into the hearts of humble people who look for truth from God. If we keep trying to speak for the Lord, we will be surprised someday to learn that we have warned, exhorted, taught, and invited with the help of the Spirit to bless lives, with power far beyond our own.

In addition to the call to teach, all of us will be sent by the Lord to succor those in need. That is another priesthood service in which we will feel the influence of the Spirit increase our power to serve. You will find yourself more able to recognize pain and worry in the faces of people. Names or the faces of people in your quorum will come into your mind with the impression that they are in need.

Bishops have that feeling come to them during the night and each time they sit on the stand looking at the members of their ward or thinking of those who are not there. It can happen to them when they find themselves near a hospital or a care center. More than once I have heard the words when I walked in the door of a hospital: "I knew you would come."

We need not worry about knowing the right thing to say or do when we get there. The love of God and the Holy Spirit may be

I urge all of us, young and old, who are called to speak in a meeting in the name of the Lord to dismiss our feelings of self-doubt and inadequacy. We don't have to use soaring language or convey deep insights. Simple words of testimony will do.

enough. When I was a young man I feared that I would not know what to do or to say to people in great need.

Once I was at the hospital bedside of my father as he seemed near death. I heard a commotion among the nurses in the hallway. Suddenly, President Spencer W. Kimball walked into the room and sat in a chair on the opposite side of the bed from me. I thought to myself, "Now here is my chance to watch and listen to a master at going to those in pain and suffering."

President Kimball said a few words of greeting, asked my father if he had received a priesthood blessing, and then, when Dad said that he had, the prophet sat back in his chair.

I waited for a demonstration of the comforting skills I felt I lacked and so much needed. After perhaps five minutes of watching the two of them simply smiling silently at each other, I saw President Kimball rise and say, "Henry, I think I'll go before we tire you."

I thought I had missed the lesson, but it came later. In a quiet moment with Dad after he recovered enough to go home, our conversation turned to the visit by President Kimball. Dad said quietly, "Of all the visits I had, that visit I had from him lifted my spirits the most."

President Kimball didn't speak many words of comfort, at least that I could hear, but he went with the Spirit of the Lord as his companion to give the comfort. I realize now that he was demonstrating that lesson President Thomas S. Monson taught: "How does one magnify a calling? Simply by performing the service that pertains to it."

We may be tired. Our own and our family's troubles may loom large. But there is a blessing of encouragement for those who serve under the influence of the Spirit.

That is true whether we are called to teach the gospel by the Spirit or go with the Holy Ghost to those with feeble knees and hands that hang down (see Doctrine and Covenants 81:5). Our priesthood service will be strengthened, people will be blessed, and the light of heaven will be there. The light of heaven will be there for us as well as for those we serve. We may be tired. Our own and our family's troubles may loom large. But there is a blessing of encouragement for those who serve under the influence of the Spirit.

President George Q. Cannon had more than his fair share of sorrow, opposition, and trials in his years of priesthood service. He also had experience with the Holy Ghost as his companion in difficult times and hard service. This is the assurance to us in our priesthood service, in the Church and in our families. For me the promise has been true when I have felt the Spirit in my priesthood service. "Whenever darkness fills our minds, we may know that we are not possessed of the Spirit of God. . . . When we are filled with the Spirit of God we are filled with joy, with peace, and with happiness, no matter what our circumstances may be; for it is a spirit of cheerfulness and of happiness. The Lord has given unto us the gift of the Holy Ghost. It is our privilege to have that Holy Ghost reign within us, so that from morning till night and from night till morning we shall have the joy, the light and the revelation thereof" (in Brian H. Stuy, comp., *Collected Discourses Delivered by President Wilford Woodruff, His Two Counselors, the Twelve Apostles, and Others,* 5 vols. [1987–1992], 4:137).

We can watch for that blessing of happiness and joy to come when we need it during the difficult times in our faithful priesthood service.

RISE TO YOUR CALL

Not long ago, a young man I did not know approached me in a crowded place. He said quietly but with great intensity: "Elder Eyring, I have just been called as the president of my elders quorum. What advice do you have for me?"

That young man is not alone in wanting help. Thousands of members of the Church across the earth are called every week to serve, many of them recent converts. The variety in their callings is great, and the variety of their previous Church experience is even greater. If you are the one who calls them, or trains them, or simply cares about them, as we all do, there are some things to know about how to help them succeed.

You may think first of being sure that they get a handbook, lesson manuals, or the records they are to keep. You might even give them a list of the times and the places of the meetings they are to attend. Then you might be about to tell them how their work will be evaluated, when you will notice concern in their eyes.

You see, even the newest member of the Church can sense that a call to service should be primarily a matter of the heart. It is by giving our whole hearts to the Master and keeping His commandments that we come to know Him. In time, through the power of the Atonement, our hearts are changed, and we can become like

Him. So there is a better way to help those who are called than descriptions of what they are to do.

What they will need, even more than to be trained in their duties, is to see with spiritual eyes what it means to be called to serve in the restored Church of Jesus Christ. This is the kingdom of God on the earth. Because of that, it has a power beyond any other endeavor in which humans can engage. That power depends on the faith of those called to serve in it.

And so, to everyone, man or woman, girl or boy, who has been called or who will yet be, I give you my counsel. There are a few things you must come to know are true. I will try to put them in words. Only the Lord through the Holy Ghost can put them deep in your heart. Here they are:

> *It is by giving our whole hearts to the Master and keeping His commandments that we come to know Him.*

First, you are called of God. The Lord knows you. He knows whom He would have serve in every position in His Church. He chose you. He has prepared a way so that He could issue your call. He restored the keys of the priesthood to Joseph Smith. Those keys have been passed down in an unbroken line to our current prophet. Through those keys, other priesthood servants were given keys to preside in stakes and wards, in districts and branches. It was through those keys that the Lord called you. Those keys confer a right to revelation. And revelation comes in answer to prayer. The person who was inspired to recommend you for this call didn't do it because they liked you or because they needed someone to do a particular task. They prayed and felt an answer that you were the one to be called.

The person who called you did not issue the call simply because he learned by interviewing you that you were worthy and willing to serve. He prayed to know the Lord's will for you. It was prayer and revelation to those authorized of the Lord which brought you here. Your call is an example of a source of power unique to the Lord's Church. Men and women are called of God by prophecy and by the laying on of hands by those God has authorized.

Just the way you smile or the way you offer to help someone can build their faith. And should you forget who you are, just the way you speak and the way you behave can destroy faith.

You are called to represent the Savior. Your voice to testify becomes the same as His voice, your hands to lift the same as His hands. His work is to bless His Father's spirit children with the opportunity to choose eternal life. So, your calling is to bless lives. That will be true even in the most ordinary tasks you are assigned and in moments when you might be doing something not apparently connected to your call. Just the way you smile or the way you offer to help someone can build their faith. And should you forget who you are, just the way you speak and the way you behave can destroy faith.

Your call has eternal consequences for others and for you. In the world to come, thousands may call your name blessed, even more than the people you serve here. They will be the ancestors and the descendants of those who chose eternal life because of something you said or did, or even what you were. If someone rejects the Savior's invitation because you did not do all you could have done, their sorrow will be yours. You see, there are no small callings to represent the Lord. Your call carries grave responsibility. But you need not fear, because with your call come great promises.

One of those promises is the second thing you need to know. It is that the Lord will guide you by revelation just as He called you. You must ask in faith for revelation to know what you are to do. With your call comes the promise that answers will come. But that guidance will come only when the Lord is sure you will obey. To know His will you must be committed to do it. The words "Thy will be done," written in the heart, are the window to revelation.

Pondering the scriptures will lead you to ask the right questions in prayer. And just as surely as the heavens were opened to Joseph Smith after he pondered the scriptures in faith, God will answer your prayers and He will lead you by the hand.

The answer comes by the Holy Spirit. You will need that guidance often. To have the Holy Ghost as your companion you must be worthy, cleansed by the Atonement of Jesus Christ. So, your obedience to the commandments, your desire to do His will, and your asking in faith will determine how clearly the Master can guide you by answers to your prayers.

Often the answers will come as you study the scriptures. They contain accounts of what the Lord did in His mortal ministry and the guidance He has given His servants. They have doctrine in them which will apply in every time and every situation. Pondering the scriptures will lead you to ask the right questions in prayer. And just as surely as the heavens were opened to Joseph Smith after he pondered the scriptures in faith, God will answer your prayers and He will lead you by the hand.

There is a third thing you need to know: Just as God called you and will guide you, He will magnify you. You will need that magnification. Your calling will surely bring opposition. You are in the Master's service. You are His representative. Eternal lives depend on you. He faced opposition, and He said that facing opposition would be the lot of those He called. The forces arrayed against you will try not only to frustrate your work but to bring you down. The Apostle Paul described it this way: "For we wrestle not against flesh and blood, but against principalities, against powers, against the rulers of the darkness of this world" (Ephesians 6:12).

There will be times when you will feel overwhelmed. One of the ways you will be attacked is with the feeling that you are inadequate. Well, you are inadequate to answer a call to represent God with only your own powers. But you have access to more than your natural capacities, and you do not work alone.

The Lord will magnify what you say and what you do in the eyes of the people you serve. He will send the Holy Ghost to manifest to them that what you spoke was true. What you say and do will carry hope and give direction to people far beyond your natural abilities and your own understanding. That miracle has been a mark of the Lord's Church in every dispensation. It is so much a part of your call that you may begin to take it for granted.

The day of your release will teach you a great lesson. On the day I was released as a bishop, one of the ward members came to my home afterward and said: "I know you are no longer my bishop, but could we talk just one more time? You have always spoken words I needed and given me such good counsel. The new bishop doesn't know me the way you do. Could we just talk one more time?"

Reluctantly I agreed. The member sat down in a chair opposite mine. It seemed to be just as it had been in the hundreds of times I had interviewed members of the ward as a judge in Israel. The conversation began. There came the moment when counsel was needed. I waited for the ideas, the words, and the feelings to flow into my mind, as they always had.

Nothing came. In my heart and mind there was only silence. After a few moments, I said: "I'm sorry. I appreciate your kindness and your trust. But I'm afraid I can't help you."

When you are released from your calling, you will learn what I learned then. God magnifies those He calls, even in what may seem to you a small or inconspicuous service. You will have the gift of seeing your service magnified. Give thanks while that gift is yours. You will appreciate its worth more than you can imagine when it is gone.

The Lord will not only magnify the power of your efforts. He will work with you Himself. His voice to four missionaries, called through the Prophet Joseph Smith to a difficult task, gives courage to everyone He calls in His kingdom: "And I myself will go with them and be in their midst; and I am their advocate with the Father, and nothing shall prevail against them" (Doctrine and Covenants 32:3).

Because the Savior is a resurrected and glorified being, He is not physically with every one of His servants at every moment. But He is perfectly aware of them and their circumstance and able to intervene with His power. That is why He can promise you: "Whoso receiveth you, there I will be also, for I will go before your face. I will be on your right hand and on your left, and my Spirit shall be in your hearts, and mine angels round about you, to bear you up" (Doctrine and Covenants 84:88).

There is yet another way the Lord will magnify you in your call to His service. You will feel at some time, perhaps at many times, that you cannot do all you feel you must. The heavy weight of your responsibilities will seem too great. You will worry that you can't spend more time with your family. You will wonder how you can find the time and the energy to meet your responsibilities beyond your family and your calling. You may feel discouragement and even guilt after you have done all you could to meet all your obligations. I have had such days and such nights. Let me tell you what I have learned.

It is this: If I only think of my own performance, my sadness deepens. But when I remember that the Lord promised that His power would go with me, I begin to look for evidence of what He has done in the lives of the people I am to serve. I pray to see with spiritual eyes the effects of His power.

You can have the utmost assurance that your power will be multiplied many times by the Lord. All He asks is that you give your best effort and your whole heart. Do it cheerfully and with the prayer of faith. Your efforts will be magnified in the lives of the people you serve.

Then, invariably, the faces of people flood back into my memory. I remember the shine in the eyes of my child whose heart was softened, the tears of happiness on the face of a girl on the back row of a Sunday School class I was teaching, or a problem that was resolved before I had time to get to it. I know then that I have done enough for the promise made by Joseph Smith to be fulfilled once again: "Let us cheerfully do all things that lie in our power;

and then may we stand still, with the utmost assurance, to see the salvation of God, and for his arm to be revealed" (Doctrine and Covenants 123:7).

You can have the utmost assurance that your power will be multiplied many times by the Lord. All He asks is that you give your best effort and your whole heart. Do it cheerfully and with the prayer of faith. The Father and His Beloved Son will send the Holy Ghost as your companion to guide you. Your efforts will be magnified in the lives of the people you serve. And when you look back on what may now seem trying times of service and sacrifice, the sacrifice will have become a blessing, and you will know that you have seen the arm of God lifting those you served for Him, and lifting you.

ACT IN ALL DILIGENCE

President Brigham Young made a powerful promise to the priesthood holder who is diligent over a lifetime: "An individual who holds a share in the Priesthood, and continues faithful to his calling, who delights himself continually in doing the things God requires at his hands, and continues through life in the performance of every duty will secure to himself not only the privilege of receiving, but the knowledge [of] how to receive the things of God, that he may know the mind of God continually" (*Teachings of Presidents of the Church: Brigham Young* [1997], 128).

I remembering seeing one new deacon start on that path of diligence. His father showed me a diagram his son had created that showed every row in their chapel, a number for each deacon who would be assigned to pass the sacrament, and their route through the chapel to serve the sacrament to the members. The father and I smiled to think that a boy, without being asked to do it, would make a plan to be sure he would succeed in his priesthood service.

I recognized in his diligence the pattern from the *Duty to God* booklet. It is to learn what the Lord expects of you, make a plan to do it, act on your plan with diligence, and then share with others how your experience changed you and blessed others.

The deacon made that diagram to be sure that he would be able to do what the Lord had called him to do. At the start of his priesthood service, the Lord was teaching him to delight in continually "doing the things God requires at his hands" (*Teachings: Brigham Young,* 128).

I also had a sweet experience watching a man near the end of his priesthood service in this life. He had been a bishop twice. His first call as a bishop, years before I met him, had been when he was young. Now he was old, released for the second time as a bishop. His increasing physical limitations made any priesthood service very difficult.

Yet he had a plan to act in diligence. He sat every Sunday he could get to church on the row nearest the door where most of the people would enter for the sacrament meeting. He got there early to be sure a seat was vacant. Each person arriving could see his look of love and welcome, just as they did when he sat on the stand as their bishop. His influence warmed and lifted us because we knew something of the price he paid to serve. His task as a bishop was finished; his priesthood service did not end.

You have seen such examples of great priesthood servants. That example begins with their learning to know whose service they are in and for what purpose. When that goes down into their hearts, it makes all the difference.

To the young men of the Aaronic Priesthood, I would say that you will become more diligent as you feel the magnitude of the trust God has placed in you. There is a message from the First Presidency for you in that *Duty to God* booklet: "Heavenly Father has great trust and confidence in you and has an important mission for you to fulfill. He will help you as you turn to Him in prayer, listen for the promptings of the Spirit, obey the commandments, and keep the covenants that you have made" (*Fulfilling My Duty to God: For Aaronic Priesthood Holders* [booklet, 2010], 5).

John the Baptist returned to earth to restore the priesthood you young men hold. He held the keys of the Aaronic Priesthood. It was John to whom Jesus turned to be baptized. John knew who called him. He said to the Lord, "I have need to be baptized of thee" (Matthew 3:14).

John knew that the priesthood of Aaron "holds the keys of the ministering of angels, and of the gospel of repentance, and of baptism by immersion for the remission of sins" when the Lord sent him to ordain Joseph Smith and Oliver Cowdery on May 15, 1829 (see Doctrine and Covenants 13:1). He knew who called him and for what glorious purpose he was sent.

Your priesthood allows you to offer the sacrament of the Lord's Supper to the members of His Church today. That is the same privilege the Savior granted the Twelve Apostles in His mortal ministry. He did it again when He called twelve disciples after His Resurrection to lead His Church.

The Lord Himself, as described in the Book of Mormon, provided the emblems of His infinite sacrifice and administered them to the people. Think of Him and how He honors you when you perform your priesthood service. As you remember Him, you will be

> *The Lord Himself, as described in the Book of Mormon, provided the emblems of His infinite sacrifice and administered them to the people. Think of Him and how He honors you when you perform your priesthood service. As you remember Him, you will be determined to perform that sacred service, as nearly as you can, as well and faithfully as He did.*

determined to perform that sacred service, as nearly as you can, as well and faithfully as He did (see 3 Nephi 20:3–9).

That can become a pattern in your life that will increase your power to be diligent in every priesthood service for which the Lord is preparing you and to which He will call you. That determination will help you prepare for receiving the Melchizedek Priesthood, which was anciently called "the Holy Priesthood, after the Order of the Son of God" (Doctrine and Covenants 107:3; see also Alma 13:1–9).

Like the Aaronic Priesthood, the Melchizedek Priesthood is more than a trust to do what the Lord would do. It is an invitation to become as He is. Here is His promise:

"For whoso is faithful unto the obtaining these two priest-hoods of which I have spoken, and the magnifying their calling, are sanctified by the Spirit unto the renewing of their bodies.

"They become the sons of Moses and of Aaron and the seed of Abraham, and the church and kingdom, and the elect of God.

"And also all they who receive this priesthood receive me, saith the Lord;

"For he that receiveth my servants receiveth me;

"And he that receiveth me receiveth my Father;

"And he that receiveth my Father receiveth my Father's king-dom; therefore all that my Father hath shall be given unto him" (Doctrine and Covenants 84:33–38).

There is a pattern by which all priesthood holders are lifted to that glorious blessing. One place in scripture where the Lord gives the pattern for us is in the 107th section of the Doctrine and Covenants:

"Wherefore, now let every man learn his duty, and to act in the office in which he is appointed, in all diligence.

"He that is slothful shall not be counted worthy to stand, and he that learns not his duty and shows himself not approved shall not be counted worthy to stand. Even so. Amen" (Doctrine and Covenants 107:99–100).

We are to learn our duty from the Lord, and then we are to act in all diligence, never being lazy or slothful. The pattern is simple but not easy to follow. We are so easily distracted. Studying the daily news can appear more interesting than the priesthood lesson manual. Sitting down to rest can be more attractive than making appointments to visit those who need our priesthood service.

When I find myself drawn away from my priesthood duties by other interests and when my body begs for rest, I give to myself this rallying cry: "Remember Him."

When I find myself drawn away from my priesthood duties by other interests and when my body begs for rest, I give to myself this rallying cry: "Remember Him." The Lord is our perfect example of diligence in priesthood service. He is our captain. He called us. He goes before us. He chose us to follow Him and to bring others with us. I remember His example in the days before.

Out of love for His Father and for us, He allowed Himself to suffer beyond the capacity of mortal man. He told us some of what that infinite sacrifice required of Him. You remember the words:

"For behold, I, God, have suffered these things for all, that they might not suffer if they would repent;

"But if they would not repent they must suffer even as I;

"Which suffering caused myself, even God, the greatest of all, to tremble because of pain, and to bleed at every pore, and to suffer both body and spirit—and would that I might not drink the bitter cup, and shrink—

"Nevertheless, glory be to the Father, and I partook and finished my preparations unto the children of men" (Doctrine and Covenants 19:16–19).

From the cross on Calvary, the Savior announced, "It is finished" (John 19:30). Then His spirit left His body, and His mortal remains were placed lovingly in a tomb. He taught us a lesson by what He did in three days in the spirit world, before His Resurrection, which I remember whenever I am tempted to feel that I have finished some hard task in His service and deserve a rest.

The Savior's example gives me courage to press on. His labors in mortality were finished, but He entered the spirit world determined to continue His glorious work to save souls. He organized the work of the faithful spirits to rescue those who could still be made partakers of the mercy made possible by His atoning sacrifice. Remember the words from the 138th section of the Doctrine and Covenants:

"But behold, from among the righteous, he organized his forces and appointed messengers, clothed with power and authority, and commissioned them to go forth and carry the light of the gospel to them that were in darkness, even to all the spirits of men; and thus was the gospel preached to the dead.

"And the chosen messengers went forth to declare the acceptable day of the Lord and proclaim liberty to the captives who were bound, even unto all who would repent of their sins and receive the gospel" (Doctrine and Covenants 138:30–31).

Whenever we remember Him, it becomes easier to resist the temptation to want a rest from our priesthood labors. Because of His example we will endure to the end of the tasks He gives us in this life and be committed to do the will of His Father forever, as He was and is.

This is the Lord's Church. He called us and trusted us even in the weaknesses He knew we had. He knew the trials we would face. By faithful service and through His Atonement, we can come to want what He wants and be what we must be to bless those we serve for Him. As we serve Him long enough and with diligence, we will be changed. We can become ever more like Him.

I have seen evidence of that miracle in the lives of His servants. I saw it one day in the living room of a faithful priesthood holder. I had known him as a deacon, a father, a bishop, and a member of a stake presidency. I had observed for decades his diligence in serving God's children with his priesthood.

His family was gathered around him in his living room. He was smiling, dressed in a white shirt, suit, and tie. I was surprised, since I was there because I had been told that he was in the midst of painful medical treatments that had not yet cured him.

The Lord knew the trials we would face. By faithful service and through His Atonement, we can come to want what He wants and be what we must be to bless those we serve for Him.

Yet he had greeted me as he must have greeted hundreds of other visitors over a lifetime of priesthood service, smiling. I had come to help him in the trials he faced, but as so often happens in priesthood service, I was helped and I learned.

We sat and chatted pleasantly. He told me how his father had tended to my mother as she approached death. I had not known that. I realized then that he had learned as a boy from his diligent priesthood father how to give succor. That thought made me grateful for the times I had taken my little boys with me on priesthood visits to comfort and bless.

After a few minutes, he asked quietly, "Would it be appropriate to ask if you could give me a blessing?" His former stake president, with whom he had served for years, anointed his head with oil consecrated by the power of the Melchizedek Priesthood.

As I sealed the blessing, I was taught by the Holy Ghost at least part of what the Lord had already done for this faithful priesthood holder. He was clean, his sins washed away. His nature had been changed to want what the Savior wanted. He had no fear of death. The desire of his heart was to live to give service to his family and to others of Heavenly Father's children who needed him.

I walked out into the night grateful to have witnessed the Lord's kindness to His unfailingly diligent priesthood servants. He changes their hearts to want what He wants and to act as He would act.

Plead that the Spirit will show you what the Lord wants you to do. Plan to do it. Promise Him to obey. Act with determination until you have done what He asked.

I invite you to ponder deeply and diligently in the scriptures and in the words of living prophets. Persist in prayer for the Holy Ghost to reveal to you the nature of God the Father and His Beloved Son. Plead that the Spirit will show you what the Lord wants you to do. Plan to do it. Promise Him to obey. Act with determination until you have done what He asked. And then pray to give thanks for the opportunity to serve and to know what you might do next.

A CHILD AND A DISCIPLE

All of us who are under the baptismal covenant have promised to offer the gospel to others (see Doctrine and Covenants 88:81; Mosiah 18:9). Sometimes, fear of rejection or of giving offense looms before us like an impassable obstacle. Yet some members clear that barrier with ease. I have observed them carefully in my travels. I can picture some of them now.

Saturday is a market day across the world. In the countryside of Ghana, in Ecuador, and in the Philippine Islands, countless people bring the produce of their farms and their handicrafts to a town to sell. They talk with those they meet on the road. And they visit with those near them as they wait for someone to buy. Much of the talk is about the struggles of existence, of breaking out of poverty, and sometimes about danger.

Among those on the roads and in the markets are Latter-day Saints. Much of their talk with those they meet would be the same as you would hear anywhere in the world. "Where are you from?" "Is that your son with you?" "How many children do you have?" But there will be a difference in the Latter-day Saints. It would be noticeable in their eyes as much as in their words. They listen carefully with the look of someone who cares about the answers to questions and who cares about the person.

If the conversation lasts more than a few minutes, it would

turn to things that matter deeply to both of them. They would talk of what they believe brings happiness and what brings sadness. And the talk would turn to hopes for this life and the next. The Latter-day Saint would express quiet assurance. Not every time, but sometimes, the Latter-day Saint would be asked, "Why are you so much at peace?" "How do you know these things you say you know?"

And then there would come a quiet answer. Perhaps it would be about Heavenly Father and His Son, Jesus Christ, appearing to the young boy Joseph Smith. It might be about the resurrected Savior's loving ministry, as described in the Book of Mormon, to common people who had faith in Him and who loved Him as we do.

"How could I become better at sharing my faith with those who do not yet feel what I feel?" It is a question for each of us who are members. The answer to that question is at the heart of the harvest which will come.

If you could hear such a conversation, which reaches spiritual things in a marketplace or on a street, you might ask: "How could I do that? How could I become better at sharing my faith with those who do not yet feel what I feel?" It is a question for each of us who are members. That same question is on the mind of every bishop and branch president in the Church who now has the charge to lead missionary work among his people. The answer to that question is at the heart of the harvest which will come.

I've studied carefully and prayerfully some who are remarkably faithful and effective witnesses of the Savior and His Church. Their stories are inspiring. One humble man was called as the president of a tiny branch. There were so few members he could not see how the branch could function. He walked into a grove of trees to pray. He asked God what he should do. An answer came. He and the few members began inviting friends to join with them. In a year, hundreds had come into the waters of baptism and become fellow citizens in the Lord's Church.

I know a man who travels almost every week in his work. On any day there are missionaries somewhere in the world teaching someone he met. There is another man who seems undeterred by how many he must speak to before any of them wish to be taught by the missionaries. He doesn't count the cost in his effort but only the happiness of those whose lives are changed.

There is no single pattern in what they do. There is no common technique. Some always carry a Book of Mormon to give away. Others set a date to find someone for the missionaries to teach. Another has found questions which draw out feelings about what matters most in life to a person. Each has prayed to know what to do. They each seem to get a different answer, suited especially to them and to the people they meet.

But in one way they are all alike. It is this: they have a common way of seeing who they are. They can do what they have been inspired to do because of who they are. To do what we are to do, we will have to become like them in at least two ways. First, they feel that they are the beloved children of a loving Heavenly Father. Because of that they turn to Him easily and often in prayer. They expect to receive His personal direction. They obey in meekness and humility, as the children of a perfect parent. He is close to them.

Second, they are the grateful disciples of the resurrected Jesus Christ. They know for themselves that the Atonement is real and necessary for all. They have felt cleansed through baptism by those in authority and the receipt of the Holy Ghost for themselves. And because of the peace they have experienced, they are like the sons of Mosiah, "desirous that salvation should be declared to every creature, for they could not bear that any human soul should perish; yea, even the very thoughts that any soul should endure endless torment did cause them to quake and tremble" (Mosiah 28:3).

Those who speak easily and often of the restored gospel prize what it has meant to them. They think of that great blessing often. It is the memory of the gift they have received which makes them eager for others to receive it. They have felt the love of the Savior. For them these words are their daily, hourly reality:

"There is no fear in love; but perfect love casteth out fear: because fear hath torment. He that feareth is not made perfect in love.

"We love him, because he first loved us" (1 John 4:18–19).

Even having felt that love, the true disciple sometimes feels anxiety. The Apostle John was clear about that: fear will be gone when we are made *perfect* in love. We can pray for that gift of perfect love. We can pray with confidence that we can feel the Savior's love for us and for all we meet. He loved us and them enough to pay the price of all our sins. It is one thing to believe that. It is something far more to have our hearts changed to feel it every moment. The command to pray to feel the Savior's love is also a promise:

"Wherefore, my beloved brethren, if ye have not charity, ye are

> *Those who speak easily and often of the restored gospel prize what it has meant to them. They think of that great blessing often. It is the memory of the gift they have received which makes them eager for others to receive it.*

nothing, for charity never faileth. Wherefore, cleave unto charity, which is the greatest of all, for all things must fail—

"But charity is the pure love of Christ, and it endureth forever; and whoso is found possessed of it at the last day, it shall be well with him.

"Wherefore, my beloved brethren, pray unto the Father with all the energy of heart, that ye may be filled with this love, which he hath bestowed upon all who are true followers of his Son, Jesus Christ; that ye may become the sons of God; that when he shall appear we shall be like him, for we shall see him as he is; that we may have this hope; that we may be purified even as he is pure" (Moroni 7:46–48).

The Lord trusts His true disciples. He sends prepared people to His prepared servants. You have had the experience, as have I, of meeting people where you were sure the meeting could not have been by chance.

I have a friend who prays every day to meet someone who is prepared to receive the gospel. He carries with him a copy of the Book of Mormon. The night before a short trip recently, he decided not to take a copy with him but instead to carry what is called a pass-along card. But in the morning, a spiritual impression came: "Take a Book of Mormon with you." He put one in his bag.

A woman he knew sat next to him on the plane, and he wondered, "Is this the one?" She rode with him again on the return trip. Now he thought, "How should I bring the gospel up?"

Instead, she said to him, "You pay tithing to your Church, don't you?" He said that he did. She said that she was supposed to pay tithing to her church but she didn't. And then she said, "What is this about the Book of Mormon?" He explained that it was scripture, another witness of Jesus Christ, translated by the Prophet Joseph Smith. She seemed interested. So he reached down into his bag and said: "I was impressed to bring this book with me. I think it is for you."

She began to read it. As they parted, she said, "You and I are going to have to have more conversations about this." What my friend could not know, but God did, was that she was looking for a church. God knew she had watched my friend and wondered what about his church made him so happy. God knew she would ask about the Book of Mormon, and He knew she would be willing to be taught by the missionaries. She was prepared. So was my friend. And so can you and I be.

Your worthiness and your desire will shine in your face and your eyes. You will be excited about the Lord's Church and His work, and it will show. You will be His disciple twenty-four hours a day in every situation. You won't need to build up your courage for one great moment to speak to someone and then retreat. The fact that most people are not interested in the restored gospel will have little bearing on what you do and say. Speaking what you believe will be part of what you are.

My father was like that. He was a scientist. He lectured to audiences in countries around the world. Once I read a talk he had given to a large scientific convention. In it, he referred to creation and a Creator as he talked about his science. I knew that few, if any, in that audience would have shared his faith. So I said to him with wonder and admiration, "Dad, you bore your testimony." He looked at me with surprise on his face and said, "Did I?"

He had not even known that he was being brave. He simply said what he knew was true. When he bore testimony, even those who rejected it knew it came not by design but because it was part of him. He was what he was, wherever he was.

That is the mark of every person who is bold and effective in sharing the gospel. They see themselves as children of a loving, living Father in Heaven. And they see themselves as disciples of Jesus Christ. It takes no discipline for them to pray. They do it naturally. It is no special effort to remember the Savior. His love for them and theirs for Him is always with them. That is who they are and how they see themselves and see those around them.

Now that may seem to us to require a great change, but we can be confident that it will come. The change in individual members is happening across the Church in every nation. This is the great time foreseen by prophets since the Creation. The restored gospel will go to every nation. The Savior sent these words to the Prophet Joseph Smith:

Whatever tumults occur, we can know that God will set bounds to fulfill His promises. He, not just men, has the ultimate control of nations and of events to allow His purposes to be fulfilled.

"I have sent forth mine angel flying through the midst of heaven, having the everlasting gospel, who hath appeared unto some and hath committed it unto man, who shall appear unto many that dwell on the earth.

"And this gospel shall be preached unto every nation, and kindred, and tongue, and people" (Doctrine and Covenants 133:36–37).

Whatever tumults occur, we can know that God will set bounds to fulfill His promises. He, not just men, has the ultimate control of nations and of events to allow His purposes to be fulfilled. Among every people and every nation there will be raised up those who serve with absolute assurance that they are children of God and who have become purified disciples of the resurrected Christ in His Church.

A few years ago I spoke to the missionaries in the training

center in Japan. I promised them then that a great day would dawn in that nation. I said that there would be a great increase in the members speaking eagerly to those they met of their testimony of the restored gospel. My thought then was that the courage to speak would come from an increased admiration for the Church in that land. I know now that the great miracle, a mighty change, will come inside the members, not in the world around them.

They and members across the earth will love and listen and talk and testify out of changed hearts. Bishops and branch presidents will lead them by example. The harvest of souls will be great, and it will be safe in the Lord's hands (see Doctrine and Covenants 50:41–42).

To be part of that miracle, you must not wait until you feel closer to Heavenly Father or until you are sure that you have been purified through the Atonement of Jesus Christ. Pray for the chance to encounter people who sense there could be something better in their lives. Pray to know what you should do to help them. Your prayers will be answered. You will meet people prepared by the Lord. You will find yourself feeling and saying things beyond your past experience. And then in time you will feel yourself drawing closer to your Heavenly Father, and you will feel the cleansing and the forgiveness the Savior promises His faithful witnesses. And you will feel His approval, knowing you have done what He asked of you, because He loves you and trusts you.

OUR HEARTS KNIT
AS ONE

The Lord's prophets have always called for unity. I have heard it from every prophet of God in my lifetime. A plea for unity was the last message I remember from President David O. McKay. The need for that gift to be granted to us and the challenge to maintain it will grow greater in the days ahead, in which we will be prepared as a people for our glorious destiny.

We see increased conflict between peoples in the world around us. Those divisions and differences could infect us. But a great day of unity is coming. The Lord Jehovah will return to live with those who have become His people and will find them united, of one heart, unified with Him and with our Heavenly Father.

We are doing better as Latter-day Saints. Fathers and mothers are pleading for unity in their homes, and those prayers are being answered. Families are praying together night and morning. I was invited to kneel at bedtime with a family when I was a guest in their home. The smallest child was asked to be voice. He prayed like a patriarch for every person in the family, by name. I opened my eyes for an instant to see the faces of the other children and the parents. I could tell that they were joining their faith and their hearts in that little boy's prayer.

Some Relief Society sisters recently prayed together as they prepared to visit for the first time a young widow whose husband died suddenly. They wanted to know what to do and how to work together to help prepare the home for family and friends who would come at the time of the funeral. They needed to know what words of comfort they could speak for the Lord. An answer to their prayer came. When they arrived at the house, each sister moved to complete a task. The house was ready so quickly that some sisters regretted not being able to do more. Words of comfort were spoken which fit perfectly together. They had given the Lord's service as one, hearts knit together.

The miracle of unity is being granted to us as we pray and work for it in the Lord's way. Our hearts will be knit together in unity. God has promised that blessing to His faithful Saints whatever their differences in background and whatever conflict rages around them.

You have seen evidence, as I have, that we are moving toward becoming one. The miracle of unity is being granted to us as we pray and work for it in the Lord's way. Our hearts will be knit together in unity. God has promised that blessing to His faithful Saints whatever their differences in background and whatever conflict rages around them. He was praying for us as well as His disciples when He asked His Father that we might be one (see John 17:21; see also Doctrine and Covenants 50:43; 93:3).

The reason that we pray and ask for that blessing is the same reason the Father is granting it. We know from experience that joy comes when we are blessed with unity. We yearn, as spirit children of our Heavenly Father, for that joy which we once had with Him in the life before this one. His desire is to grant us that sacred wish for unity out of His love for us.

He cannot grant it to us as individuals. The joy of unity He wants so much to give us is not solitary. We must seek it and qualify for it with others. It is not surprising then that God urges us to gather so that He can bless us. He wants us to gather into families. He has established classes, wards, and branches and commanded us to meet together often. In those gatherings, which God has designed for us, lies our great opportunity. We can pray and work for the unity that will bring us joy and multiply our power to serve.

To the Three Nephites, the Savior promised joy in unity with Him as their final reward after their faithful service. He said, "Ye shall have fulness of joy; and ye shall sit down in the kingdom of my Father; yea, your joy shall be full, even as the Father hath given me fulness of joy; and ye shall be even as I am, and I am even as the Father; and the Father and I are one" (3 Nephi 28:10).

The Lord has given us guides to know what to do to receive the blessing and joy of ever-increasing unity. The Book of Mormon recounts a time of success. It was in the days of Alma at the Waters of Mormon. What the people did in those difficult and dangerous circumstances gives us both a guide and encouragement.

Everything Alma and his people were inspired to do was pointed at helping people choose to have their hearts changed through the Atonement of Jesus Christ. That is the only way God can grant the blessing of being of one heart.

In Mosiah we read:

"And they were called the church of God, or the church of Christ, from that time forward. And it came to pass that whosoever was baptized by the power and authority of God was added to his church. . . .

"And he commanded them that they should teach nothing save

it were the things which he had taught, and which had been spoken by the mouth of the holy prophets.

"Yea, even he commanded them that they should preach nothing save it were repentance and faith on the Lord, who had redeemed his people.

"And he commanded them that there should be no contention one with another, but that they should look forward with one eye, having one faith and one baptism, having their hearts knit together in unity and in love one towards another.

"And thus he commanded them to preach. And thus they became the children of God" (Mosiah 18:17, 19–22).

That is why Alma commanded the people to teach faith and repentance. That is why my children came to expect in every lesson in family night that I would find a way to encourage someone to testify of the Savior and His mission. Sometimes the parents did it. On our best nights we found a way to encourage the children to do it, either by presenting the lesson or answering questions. When testimony about the Savior was borne, the Holy Ghost verified it. On those nights we felt our hearts being knit together.

Revelation is the only way we can know how to follow the will of the Lord together. It requires light from above. The Holy Ghost will testify to our hearts, and the hearts of those gathered around with us, what He would have us do.

In addition to ordinances there are principles we are following as a people which are leading to greater unity.

One of those principles is revelation. Revelation is the only way we can know how to follow the will of the Lord together. It requires light from above. The Holy Ghost will testify to our hearts, and the hearts of those gathered around with us, what He would have us do. And it is by keeping His commandments that we can have our hearts knit together as one.

A second principle to guide our progress to become one is to be humble. Pride is the great enemy of unity. You have seen and felt its terrible effects. Just days ago I watched as two people—good people—began with a mild disagreement. It started as a discussion of what was true but became a contest about who was right. Voices became gradually louder. Faces became a little more flushed. Instead of talking about the issue, people began talking about themselves, giving evidence why their view, given their great ability and background, was more likely to be right.

You would have felt alarm as I did. We have seen the life-destroying effects of such tragic conflict. You and I know people who left the fellowship of the Saints over injured pride.

Happily I am seeing more and more skillful peacemakers who calm troubled waters before harm is done. You could be one of those peacemakers, whether you are in the conflict or an observer.

One way I have seen it done is to search for anything on which we agree. To be that peacemaker, you need to have the simple faith that as children of God, with all our differences, it is likely that in a strong position we take, there will be elements of truth. The great peacemaker, the restorer of unity, is the one who finds a way to help people see the truth they share. That truth they share is always greater and more important to them than their differences. You can help yourself and others to see that common ground if you ask for help from God and then act. He will answer your prayer to help restore peace, as He has mine.

That same principle applies as we build unity with people who are from vastly different backgrounds. The children of God have more in common than they have differences. And even the differences can be seen as an opportunity. God will help us see a difference in someone else not as a source of irritation but as a contribution. The Lord can help you see and value what another person brings which you lack. More than once the Lord has helped me see His kindness in giving me association with someone whose difference from me was just the help I needed. That has been the Lord's way of adding something I lacked to serve Him better.

That leads to another principle of unity. It is to speak well of each other. Think of the last time you were asked what you thought about how someone else was doing in your family or in the Church. There are times we must judge others. Sometimes we are required to pronounce such judgments. But more often we can make a choice. For instance, suppose someone asks you what you think of the new bishop.

The great peacemaker, the restorer of unity, is the one who finds a way to help people see the truth they share. That truth they share is always greater and more important to them than their differences.

As we get better and better at forging unity, we will think of a scripture when we hear that question: "And now, my brethren, seeing that ye know the light by which ye may judge, which light is the light of Christ, see that ye do not judge wrongfully; for with that same judgment which ye judge ye shall also be judged" (Moroni 7:18).

Realizing that you see others in an imperfect light will make you likely to be a little more generous in what you say. In addition to that scripture, you might remember your mother saying—mine did—"If you can't say anything good about a person, don't say anything at all."

That will help you look for what is best in the bishop's performance and character. The Savior, as your loving judge, will surely do that as He judges your performance and mine. The scripture and what you heard from your mother may well lead you to describe what is best in the bishop's performance and his good intent. I can promise you a feeling of peace and joy when you speak generously of others in the Light of Christ. You will feel, for instance, unity with that bishop and with the person who asked your opinion, not because the bishop is perfect or because the person asking you shares your generous evaluation. It will be because the Lord will let you feel His appreciation for choosing to step away from the possibility of sowing seeds of disunity.

We must follow that same principle as the Lord gathers more and more people who are not like us. What will become more obvious to us is that the Atonement brings the same changes in all of us. We become disciples who are meek, loving, easy to be entreated, and at the same time fearless and faithful in all things. We still live in different countries, but we come into the Church through a process that changes us. We become by the gifts of the Spirit what the Apostle Paul saw:

"For through him we both have access by one Spirit unto the Father.

"Now therefore ye are no more strangers and foreigners, but fellowcitizens with the saints, and of the household of God" (Ephesians 2:18–19).

With the unity I see increasing, the Lord will be able to perform what the world will think as miraculous. The Saints can accomplish any purpose of the Lord when fully united in righteousness.

Presidents of countries, governors, and leaders of worldwide charitable organizations have praised us—in my hearing—with words like these: "Your church was the first on the ground to help when disaster came. Hundreds of your people arrived who brought everything with them which the survivors needed. They even brought their own tents and supplies. They were tireless and cheerful. They seemed to know where to go and when." Then there has come a line usually something like this: "Your church knows how to organize to get things done."

I thank them without saying that the miracle lies not in organization alone, but in the people's hearts. The Saints came in the name of the Lord to give the succor He would give. They came listening to the direction of the Lord's chosen leaders. Because their hearts were knit, they were magnified in their power.

With the unity I see increasing, the Lord will be able to perform what the world will think as miraculous. The Saints can accomplish any purpose of the Lord when fully united in righteousness.

I bear you my solemn witness that the unity we now experience will increase. God the Father lives. He hears and answers our prayers in love. The Savior Jesus Christ, resurrected and glorious, lives and reaches out to us in mercy. If we are united, striving with willing obedience to do what God would have us do, we will move together in power to go wherever God would have us go and to become what He wants us to be.

HELP FOR THE
LAST DAYS

GIFTS OF THE SPIRIT FOR HARD TIMES

We are all in the probationary test of mortality. And, wherever we live, that test will become increasingly difficult. We are in the last dispensation of time. God's prophets have seen these times for millennia. They saw that wonderful things were to happen. There was to be a restoration of the gospel of Jesus Christ. The true Church was to be brought back with prophets and apostles. The gospel was to be taken to every nation, kindred, tongue, and people. Most marvelous of all, the true Church and its members are to become worthy for the coming of the Savior to His Church and to His purified disciples.

But the true prophets also saw that in the last days Satan would rage. There would be wars and rumors of wars. That would inspire fear. The courage of many would fail. There would be great wickedness. And Satan would deceive many.

Yet, happily, many would not be overcome. And many would not be deceived. The key for each of us will be to accept and hold the gift we have been promised by God. You who are members of the true Church of Jesus Christ will remember that, after you were baptized, authorized servants of God promised you that you could receive the Holy Ghost. Some of you may have felt something happen when that ordinance was performed. Most of you have felt the effects of that promise being fulfilled in your lives. I will tell you how to recognize that gift, how to receive it every day in your life, and how it will bless you in the days ahead.

You have felt the quiet confirmation in your heart and mind that something was true. And you knew that it was inspiration from God. For some of you it may have come as the missionaries taught you before your baptism. It may have come during a talk or lesson in church. The Holy Ghost is the Spirit of Truth. You feel peace, hope, and joy when it speaks to your heart and mind that something is true. Almost always I have also felt a sensation of light. Any feeling I may have had of darkness is dispelled. And the desire to do right grows.

The Holy Ghost is the Spirit of Truth. You feel peace, hope, and joy when it speaks to your heart and mind that something is true. Almost always I have also felt a sensation of light. Any feeling I may have had of darkness is dispelled. And the desire to do right grows.

The Lord promised that having those experiences would be true for you. Here are His words, recorded in the Doctrine and Covenants:

"And now, verily, verily, I say unto thee, put your trust in that Spirit which leadeth to do good—yea, to do justly, to walk humbly, to judge righteously; and this is my Spirit.

"Verily, verily, I say unto you, I will impart unto you of my Spirit, which shall enlighten your mind, which shall fill your soul with joy" (Doctrine and Covenants 11:12–13).

The Lord also promised that those who have accepted the gift of the Holy Ghost in their lives would not be deceived. He spoke reassuringly to you and to me, who live in the times when the

Church is being made ready for the time when He comes again. Here is the promise:

"And at that day, when I shall come in my glory, shall the parable be fulfilled which I spake concerning the ten virgins.

"For they that are wise and have received the truth, and have taken the Holy Spirit for their guide, and have not been deceived—verily I say unto you, they shall not be hewn down and cast into the fire, but shall abide the day.

"And the earth shall be given unto them for an inheritance; and they shall multiply and wax strong, and their children shall grow up without sin unto salvation.

"For the Lord shall be in their midst, and his glory shall be upon them, and he will be their king and their lawgiver" (Doctrine and Covenants 45:56–59).

Those words paint a picture of the day when we may be with the Savior, who spoke of the ten virgins and of His coming again—only this time in glory. And they describe a day when we might be with Him and have His glory upon us. Of all the things to which the Holy Ghost testifies, none is more precious to us than that Jesus is the Christ, the living Son of God. And nothing is so likely to make us feel light, hope, and joy. Then it is not surprising that when we feel the influence of the Holy Ghost, we also can feel that our natures are being changed because of the Atonement of Jesus Christ. We feel an increased desire to keep His commandments, to do good, and to deal justly.

Many of you have felt that effect from your frequent experiences with the Holy Ghost. For instance, in the mission field some of you had to rely on the Spirit to have the words to teach what the people needed. More than once, and perhaps every day, you had the blessing that Nephi and Lehi had among the people in their mission:

"And it came to pass that Nephi and Lehi did preach unto the Lamanites with such great power and authority, for they had power and authority given unto them that they might speak, and they also had what they should speak given unto them—

"Therefore they did speak unto the great astonishment of the Lamanites, to the convincing them, insomuch that there were eight thousand of the Lamanites who were in the land of Zarahemla and round about baptized unto repentance, and were convinced of the wickedness of the traditions of their fathers" (Helaman 5:18–19).

Of all the things to which the Holy Ghost testifies, none is more precious to us than that Jesus is the Christ, the living Son of God. And nothing is so likely to make us feel light, hope, and joy.

Although you may not have been blessed with so miraculous a harvest, you have been given words by the Holy Ghost when you surrendered your heart to the Lord's service. At certain periods of your mission, such an experience came often. If you will think back on those times and ponder, you will also remember that the increase in your desire to obey the commandments came over you gradually. You felt less and less the tug of temptation. You felt more and more the desire to be obedient and to serve others. You felt a greater love for the people.

One of the effects of receiving a manifestation of the Holy Ghost repeatedly was that your nature changed. And so, from that faithful service to the Master, you had not only the witness of the Holy Ghost that Jesus is the Christ but you saw evidence in your own life that the Atonement is real. Such service, which brings the influence of the Holy Ghost, is an example of planting the seed, which Alma described:

"And now, behold, because ye have tried the experiment, and planted the seed, and it swelleth and sprouteth, and beginneth to grow, ye must needs know that the seed is good.

"And now, behold, is your knowledge perfect? Yea, your knowledge is perfect in that thing, and your faith is dormant; and this because you know, for ye know that the word hath swelled your souls, and ye also know that it hath sprouted up, that your understanding doth begin to be enlightened, and your mind doth begin to expand.

"O then, is not this real? I say unto you, Yea, because it is light; and whatsoever is light, is good, because it is discernible, therefore ye must know that it is good; and now behold, after ye have tasted this light is your knowledge perfect?

"Behold I say unto you, Nay; neither must ye lay aside your faith, for ye have only exercised your faith to plant the seed that ye might try the experiment to know if the seed was good.

"And behold, as the tree beginneth to grow, ye will say: Let us nourish it with great care, that it may get root, that it may grow up, and bring forth fruit unto us. And now behold, if ye nourish it with much care it will get root, and grow up, and bring forth fruit" (Alma 32:33–37).

Now, if you and I were visiting alone (I wish we could be), where you felt free to ask whatever you wanted to ask, I can imagine your saying something like this: "Oh, Brother Eyring, I've felt some of the things you have described. The Holy Ghost has touched my heart and mind from time to time. But I will need it consistently if I am not to be overcome or deceived. Is that possible? Is it possible, and, if it is, what will it take to receive that blessing?"

Well, let's start with the first part of your question. Yes, it is possible. Whenever I need that reassurance—and I need it from time to time too—I remember two brothers. Nephi and Lehi, and the other servants of the Lord laboring with them, faced fierce opposition. They were serving in an increasingly wicked world. They had to deal with terrible deceptions. So I take courage—and so can you—from the words in this one verse of Helaman. The reassurance is tucked into the account of all that happened in an entire year, almost as if to the writer it was not surprising:

"And in the seventy and ninth year there began to be much strife. But it came to pass that Nephi and Lehi, and many of their brethren who knew concerning the true points of doctrine, having many revelations daily, therefore they did preach unto the people, insomuch that they did put an end to their strife in that same year" (Helaman 11:23).

They had "many revelations daily." So, for you and for me, that answers your first question. Yes, it is possible to have the companionship of the Holy Ghost sufficiently to have many revelations daily. It will not be easy. But it is possible. What it will require will be different for each person because we start from where we are in our unique set of experiences in life. For all of us there will be at least three requirements. None of them can be gained and retained from a single experience. All of them must be constantly renewed.

First, receiving the Holy Ghost takes faith in our Heavenly Father and in His Beloved Son, Jesus Christ. A memory of a great spiritual experience some time ago, where you had confirmed to you that truth, won't be sufficient. You will need to be sure of your faith in the moment of crisis, which may come at any time day or night, when you plead for the influence of the Spirit. You must then be unshaken in your confidence that God lives, that He hears your cry for help, and that the resurrected Savior will do for you what He promised to do for His servants in His mortal ministry. You remember:

"But when the Comforter is come, whom I will send unto you from the Father, even the Spirit of truth, which proceedeth from the Father, he shall testify of me" (John 15:26).

The brothers Nephi and Lehi received many revelations daily. The record shows that they knew concerning the true points of doctrine. Of all the true doctrine, nothing is more important to you and me than the true nature of God the Father and His Son, Jesus Christ. For that I return again and again to the scriptures. For that I return again and again to prayer. For that I return again and again to partaking of the sacrament. And, above all, I come to know God and Jesus Christ best by keeping the commandments and serving in the Church. By diligent service in the Church we come not only to know the character of God but to love Him. If we follow His commands, our faith in Him will grow and we may then qualify to have His Spirit to be with us.

It is possible to have the companionship of the Holy Ghost sufficiently to have many revelations daily. It will not be easy. But it is possible.

Vibrant faith in God comes best from serving Him regularly. Not all of us have received callings to offices in the Church. Some of you may not yet be called to something in a formal way, yet every member has a multitude of opportunities to serve God. For instance, for years we have heard the phrase "every member a missionary." That is not a choice. It is a fact of our membership. Our choice is to speak to others about the gospel or not. Similarly, each member is to care for the poor among us and around us. Some of that we do privately and alone. Some we do together with other members. That is why we have fast offerings and service projects. Our choice is to decide whether to join with the Lord and His other disciples in our day as He and His disciples did during His mortal ministry.

Most of us have or may have callings as home and visiting teachers. There is in those callings great opportunity to grow in faith that the Lord sends the Holy Ghost to His humble servants. That builds faith and renews our faith in Him. I've seen it and so have many of you. I received a phone call from a distraught mother in a state far away from where I was. She told me that her unmarried daughter had moved to another city far from her home. She sensed from the little contact she had with her daughter that something was terribly wrong. The mother feared for the moral safety of her daughter. She pleaded with me to help her daughter.

I found out who the daughter's home teacher was. I called him. He was young. And yet he and his companion both had been awakened in the night with not only concern for the girl but with inspiration that she was about to make choices that would bring sadness and misery. With only the inspiration of the Spirit, they went to see her. She did not at first want to tell them anything about her situation. They pleaded with her to repent and to choose to follow the path that the Lord had set out for her and that her mother and father had taught her to follow. She realized as she listened that the only way they could have known what they knew about her life was from God. A mother's prayer had gone to Heavenly Father, and the Holy Ghost had been sent to home teachers with an errand.

More than once I have heard priesthood leaders say that they had been inspired to go to someone in need, only to find the visiting teacher or the home teacher had already been there. My wife has always been a great example in this regard. We had a bishop once who said to me, "You know, it bothers me—when I get an inspiration to go to someone, your wife has already been there." Your faith will grow as you serve the Lord in caring for Heavenly Father's children as the Lord's teacher to their home. You will have your prayers answered. You will come to know for yourself that He lives, that He loves us, and that He sends inspiration to those with even the beginnings of faith in Him and with the desire to serve Him in His Church. Stay close to the Church if you want your faith in God to grow. And as it grows, so will your ability to claim the promise you were given that you can receive the gifts of the Spirit.

Stay close to the Church if you want your faith in God to grow. And as it grows, so will your ability to claim the promise you were given that you can receive the gifts of the Spirit.

The first requirement was faith in the Lord Jesus Christ and in our Heavenly Father. A second requirement for frequent companionship and direction from the Holy Ghost is to be clean. The Spirit must withdraw from those who are not clean. You remember the sad illustration of that in the history of the people in the Book of Mormon:

"And because of their iniquity the church had begun to dwindle; and they began to disbelieve in the spirit of prophecy and in the spirit of revelation; and the judgments of God did stare them in the face.

"And they saw that they had become weak, like unto their brethren, the Lamanites, and that the Spirit of the Lord did no more preserve them; yea, it had withdrawn from them because the

Spirit of the Lord doth not dwell in unholy temples" (Helaman 4:23–24).

The path to receiving the Holy Ghost is to exercise faith in Christ unto repentance. We can become clean through qualifying for the effects of the Savior's Atonement. The covenants offered in baptism by authorized servants of God bring that cleansing. We renew our pledge to keep those covenants each time we partake of the sacrament. And the peace we all seek is the assurance that we have received forgiveness for our sins of omission or commission.

The Savior is the one who has been given the right to grant that forgiveness and to give that assurance. I have learned that the Lord gives that assurance at the time He chooses, and He does it in His own way. And I have learned to ask for it in prayer. One way He grants that assurance is through the Holy Ghost. If you have difficulty in feeling the Holy Ghost, you might wisely ponder whether there is anything for which you need to repent and receive forgiveness.

If you have felt the influence of the Holy Ghost, you may take it as evidence that the Atonement is working in your life. For that reason and many others, you would do well to put yourself in places and in tasks that invite the promptings of the Holy Ghost. Feeling the influence of the Holy Ghost works both ways: the Holy Ghost only dwells in a clean temple, and the reception of the Holy Ghost cleanses us through the Atonement of Jesus Christ. You can pray with faith to know what to do to be cleansed and thus qualified for the companionship of the Holy Ghost and the service of the Lord. And with that companionship you will be strengthened against temptation and empowered to detect deception.

A third requirement for the companionship of the Holy Ghost is pure motive. If you want to receive the gifts of the Spirit, you have to want them for the right reasons. Your purposes must be the Lord's purposes. To the degree your motives are selfish, you will find it difficult to receive those gifts of the Spirit that have been promised to you.

That fact serves both as a warning and as helpful instruction. First, the warning: God is offended when we seek the gifts of the Spirit for our own purposes rather than for His. Our selfish motives may not be obvious to us. But few of us would be so blind as the man who sought to purchase the right to the gifts of the Spirit. You remember the sad story of a man named Simon and of Peter's rebuke:

If you have felt the influence of the Holy Ghost, you may take it as evidence that the Atonement is working in your life.

"And when Simon saw that through laying on of the apostles' hands the Holy Ghost was given, he offered them money,

"Saying, Give me also this power, that on whomsoever I lay hands, he may receive the Holy Ghost.

"But Peter said unto him, Thy money perish with thee, because thou hast thought that the gift of God may be purchased with money.

"Thou hast neither part nor lot in this matter: for thy heart is not right in the sight of God.

"Repent therefore of this thy wickedness, and pray God, if perhaps the thought of thine heart may be forgiven thee.

"For I perceive that thou art in the gall of bitterness, and in the bond of iniquity.

"Then answered Simon, and said, Pray ye to the Lord for me, that none of these things which ye have spoken come upon me" (Acts 8:18–24).

Apparently Simon recognized his own corrupt motives. It may not be so easy for each of us. We almost always have more than one motive at a time. And some may be mixtures of what God wants as well as what we want. It is not easy to pull them apart.

For instance, consider yourself on the eve of a school examination or an interview for a new job. You know that the direction of the Holy Ghost could be of great help. I know from my own experience, for example, that the Holy Ghost knows some of the mathematical equations used to solve problems in thermodynamics, a branch of the sciences. I was a struggling physics student studying in a book that I still own. I keep it for historical and spiritual reasons. Halfway down a page (I could even show you where it is on the page), in the middle of some mathematics, I had a clear confirmation that what I was reading was true. It was exactly the feeling I had had come to me before as I pondered the Lord's scriptures and that I have had many times since. So I knew that the Holy Ghost understood whatever was true in what I might be asked on an examination in thermodynamics.

You can imagine that I was tempted to ask God to send me the Holy Ghost during the examination so I wouldn't need to study further. I knew that He could do it, but I did not ask Him. I felt that He would rather have me learn to pay a price in effort. He may well have sent help in the examination, but I was afraid that my motive might not be His. You have had that same choice to make often. It may have been when you were to be interviewed for a job. It may even have been when you were preparing for a talk or to teach a missionary discussion. Always there is the possibility that you may have a selfish purpose for yourself that is less important to the Lord.

For instance, I may want a good grade in a course, when He prefers that I learn how to work hard in the service of others. I may want a job because of the salary or the prestige, when He wants me to work somewhere else to bless the life of someone I don't even know yet. I might have a desire to entertain or impress you. But I have tried to suppress my desire and surrender to His.

I saw a man do that once. It changed my life. A member of the General Authorities came to speak to a conference where I was sitting on the stand. I was in the local priesthood presidency. I knew personally the struggles of the local families and the members. He, the General Authority, had just flown in from a long assignment in Europe. He was obviously tired. He stood to speak in the meeting. It seemed to me that he rambled from one subject to another. At first I felt sorry for him. I thought he was failing to give a polished sermon of the kind I knew he had delivered many times.

After a while I was thrilled to recognize that as he moved from one apparently unrelated topic to another, he was touching the need of every poor struggling member and family we were trying to help. He did not know them and their needs. But God did.

How grateful I am that his motive was not to give a great sermon or to be seen as a powerful prophet. He must have done what I hope you and I will always do. He must have prayed something like this: "Father, I need Thy help. I am tired. Please guide me with the Holy Ghost. Bless these people. I love them. I ask only that I can do Thy will to help them."

The Holy Ghost came that night. And the Lord's will was done. The General Authority had spent a lifetime feeding himself and others on the good word of God. He had served the Master faithfully. He was a special witness of Jesus Christ because he had paid the price to be one. All of that came from keeping his motives as closely tied as he could to what the Lord wanted. That made it possible for the Lord to send the whisperings of the Holy Ghost to His servant and so bless the people.

I surely don't understand all the meaning of the scriptural words "the pure love of Christ." But one meaning I do know is this: It is a gift we are promised when the Atonement of Jesus Christ has worked in us. The gift is to want what He wants. When our love is the love He feels, it is pure because He is pure. And when we feel our desire for people is moving toward being in line with His, that is one of the ways that we can know that we are being purified. When we pray for the gifts of the Spirit—and we should—one for which I pray is that I might have pure motives, to want what He wants for our Father's children and for me and to feel, as well as to say, that what I want is His will to be done.

When we pray for the gifts of the Spirit—and we should—one for which I pray is that I might have pure motives, to want what He wants for our Father's children and for me and to feel, as well as to say, that what I want is His will to be done.

I pray with all the energy of my heart that you will have your prayers answered to meet the requirements to receive the Holy Ghost. And I pray that you will endure faithful to the end and that, for you, it will be glorious.

BLESSED ARE THE PEACEMAKERS

When you look at your newspaper and your television screen you don't see much about peace. Every day the news is filled with more violence, apparently growing violence, across the world and in our own cities. Chances are, you even plan what you do at night, taking your safety into account. You hope to avoid the violence of other people.

Now, if you listen carefully, in the debates about what to do to create peace, you will hear some common themes. Interestingly, the themes remain much the same whether the question is how to gain peace in the world or in your neighborhood. One theme is disarmament. Those who see danger in bombs or in guns take comfort when any country or any group of people give up weapons. But there are those, equally sure, who argue that the only safety is to have enough bombs or guns that no one will attack you.

Another theme is that of negotiation: If we can just get people to talk with each other, then they will choose peace. And so you read about and see pictures of diplomats and secretaries of state and heads of nations flying to Geneva or somewhere else to talk. Always the media is there to tell you how it is going. They try to judge whether, because of what is negotiated, the shooting will stop or go on. But even when shooting stops, usually just for a short while, the meetings and the media move to some other place, because the shooting has started somewhere else.

Another theme in the search for peace is education: If people just knew more, if they understood better, if they were educated enough to have a better life, they would choose peace. And so we search for ways for more people to have better educations.

In that theme, the theme of education, is a key to understanding both the difficulties in most proposed solutions to violence and also the sure way to peace. The hope of ending violence by better education is that if people just understood better, they would want peace and so they would choose it. If you believe education could promote peace, you believe that anyone who could think clearly will not choose violence. But when you look at experience, both in your life and as the world has sought peace, you can see that the most devastating violence begins in thoughtful choice. Disarmament treaties are signed, and then nations, and individuals, decide that it is in their best interest to break them. So, they do, usually in secret and then finally in the open. Or, people decide that arming themselves will keep the peace, and then, quite rationally, get more arms to match what their enemy gets. And then both sides acquire so much that their own bombs and guns become as dangerous to them as are those in the hands of their enemies.

Even the proposals to build more prisons and have tougher laws and give us more law enforcement officers are based on the hope that people who would harm you will make a thoughtful choice not to try. But you know from your own experience and from observing others where that finally fails. As long as people want something for themselves enough to hurt you to get it, they will keep searching until they find a way. And you can never build a fence long enough, or high enough, or strong enough but that they will find a way around, or under, or through it.

That is why neither education, nor disarmament, nor armament, nor negotiation, nor all of them in combination are likely to create a world or a neighborhood of lasting peace. To do that, a change has to come into human hearts. The change must be in what people want. Almost everyone in the world has heard of what that change is, because it is common to religions and philosophies across the world and across the centuries. It is said differently in the scriptures and writings of others, but the words you will recognize best are these: "Therefore, all things whatsoever ye would that men should do to you, do ye even so to them, for this is the law and the prophets" (3 Nephi 14:12).

Neither education, nor disarmament, nor armament, nor negotiation, nor all of them in combination are likely to create a world or a neighborhood of lasting peace. To do that, a change has to come into human hearts.

You can see how that would work, if that change had come to your heart and to mine. If you and I both felt that way, whether we did or didn't have a gun wouldn't matter, unless you tried to give me yours because you felt I needed it to hunt for food more than you did.

We would certainly still need to negotiate when we disagreed, but our negotiations would take a very different turn. I saw two such men—changed men—negotiate for a place in a cafeteria waiting line a few years ago. One, the younger man, tried to get the older man to go ahead of him, because he thought the older man's time was more valuable than his. But the older man refused. They were negotiating their disagreement as I watched, both determined that the other would go first. I remember that the older man won his point. His name was Spencer W. Kimball. The younger man must have thought that the time of the President of the Church was more valuable than his. But I suppose President Kimball thought that the younger man's stomach needed something in it sooner than his did. There was disagreement and negotiation. But think of what a disagreement that was, and think of the smiles on their faces as they found, together, a path of peace.

Education can help you understand what is in the interests of your brothers and sisters and in your own best interests. And it can help you know how to create and to provide what will be in our best interest. The fruits of science and of other learning are enriching our lives today beyond what our ancestors, even a few generations ago, could have imagined. Much of that came from the fruits of people who sacrificed and persevered to gain education and then used its fruits in the service of others.

But knowing what is best for you and me, and even knowing how to provide it, will not necessarily change our hearts to want each other's interests as much as we want our own. That is the change which matters. And only a very special and rare education, one that the Savior Jesus Christ offers, will bring it into human hearts. And that is what we need in ourselves, in our families, in our neighborhoods, and in the world.

Now, as Latter-day Saints, we should work for peace. You remember that the Lord said, "Therefore, renounce war and proclaim peace" (Doctrine and Covenants 98:16).

So we should study out and then support whatever would reduce war and violence. But among all the proposals we may consider, only one will go to the heart of what is required for peace. Look at the very next phrase in that section of the Doctrine and Covenants, after we are commanded by God to renounce war and proclaim peace. It is just a few words—they may seem to some almost not connected to what went before, but they tell us where to look for the path to peace. Here is the whole phrase:

"Therefore, renounce war and proclaim peace, and seek diligently to turn the hearts of the children to their fathers, and the hearts of the fathers to the children" (Doctrine and Covenants 98:16).

The path away from war and violence and toward peace is in the turning of hearts. And we wisely start with a turning in feelings toward others—those closest to us, those to whom we owe the most, those upon whom we most depend, and those with whom we want to associate most often.

With all the effort and thought and caring you may give to the pursuit of peace, never stray far from seeking ways to change hearts. And start close by, in your own heart and the hearts of those close to you.

With all the effort and thought and caring you may give to the pursuit of peace, never stray far from seeking ways to change hearts. And start close by, in your own heart and the hearts of those close to you.

More than that, we know, because God has told us through His servants, the road to travel to find peace. No road leads to peace, for a person or for the world, unless it leads away from the effects of sin and Satan. Satan has always taught men and women to take what they want by taking life. I like the forthright way John Taylor, a president of the Church in this dispensation, gave us the direction to follow. He said:

"Peace is the gift of God. Do you want peace? Go to God. Do you want peace in your families? Go to God. Do you want peace to brood over your families? If you do, live your religion, and the very peace of God will dwell and abide with you, for that is where peace comes from, and it do[es]n't dwell anywhere else" (*Journal of Discourses*, 26 vols. [1854–1886], 10:56).

When President Taylor urges you to go to God for peace, he is saying more, much more, than to simply ask for it in prayer. That change in what we want, the one that will bring peace in your heart and then between people, is the natural fruit of the Atonement of Jesus Christ working in your life. President Spencer W. Kimball described our private peace this way:

"The essence of the miracle of forgiveness is that it brings peace to the previously anxious, restless, frustrated, perhaps tormented soul. In a world of turmoil and contention this is indeed a priceless gift" (*The Miracle of Forgiveness* [1969], 363).

And then, just a few pages later, he wrote, almost as if he were explaining how to follow the instruction of President Taylor:

"It is not easy to be at peace in today's troubled world. Necessarily peace is a personal acquisition . . . it can be attained only through maintaining constantly a repentant attitude, seeking forgiveness of sins both large and small, and thus coming ever closer to God. For Church members this is the essence of their preparation, their readiness to meet the Savior when he comes" (*The Miracle of Forgiveness*, 366).

How that cleansing of sin changes our hearts and moves us closer to God is described in numbers of ways in the scriptures, but one seems to me the clearest in telling you what to do to help others want to make the change and then choose to make it. This is almost like a list of instructions, and it is a simple one, one you could follow:

"And the first fruits of repentance is baptism; and baptism

cometh by faith unto the fulfilling the commandments; and the fulfilling the commandments bringeth remission of sins;

"And the remission of sins bringeth meekness, and lowliness of heart; and because of meekness and lowliness of heart cometh the visitation of the Holy Ghost, which Comforter filleth with hope and perfect love, which love endureth by diligence unto prayer, until the end shall come, when all the saints shall dwell with God" (Moroni 8:25–26).

There are words to remember there. The remission of sins brings meekness and lowliness of heart. Because of that, the Holy Ghost can come, which gives us hope and perfect love. And that love—if you ask God for help with enough faith and sincerity and often enough—will stay with you through all the troubles and hatred you will ever face. And then you will live with God.

Now, with that clear, one of the passages in Isaiah that you may sometimes pass too quickly because you think you won't understand it, makes perfect sense: "And the work of righteousness shall be peace; and the effect of righteousness quietness and assurance for ever" (Isaiah 32:17).

But you might well say, "But do I have to wait until I am perfect and the people around me are perfect before I can live in peace?" I suppose in one way the answer is, "Yes," if you mean to live in perfect peace. But there is a much happier answer, and a true one. It is this: We are promised peace in this life before we are perfect. You remember how the preface to the Book of Mormon describes its most important message:

"The crowning event recorded in the Book of Mormon is the personal ministry of the Lord Jesus Christ among the Nephites soon after His resurrection. It puts forth the doctrines of the gospel, outlines the plan of salvation, and tells men what they must do to gain peace in this life and eternal salvation in the life to come" (Introduction, paragraph 3).

I testify to you that you can taste peace in this life. God grants us peace as we go along the road to perfection. Let me tell you how I know some things you can do to make it more likely that those around you will find the peace the gospel brings. The reason I can do this is that people around me have helped me make choices that brought changes and peace to me. Now, to be honest with you, I also know what to recommend to you because when those around me didn't do these things we'll talk about, there was less peace, and sometimes sadness for me. That wasn't because the people around me made me sad, but because without these influences we'll talk about, I was less likely to make the choices that would have brought me peace.

> *I testify to you that you can taste peace in this life. God grants us peace as we go along the road to perfection.*

I can imagine a question forming in your mind. It goes something like this: "Wait a minute, Brother Eyring, are you saying that my living the gospel depends on help from people around me? Don't you know that I am nearly alone in trying to live the gospel?"

I know that many of you struggle with little help from those around you. No, of course you are not dependent, and neither am I, on having people around us to help. We are all responsible for our choices. And God will not leave us so alone that we cannot live the gospel of Jesus Christ. He never gives a commandment without preparing the way for us to keep it. And I am like you: I want to be strong enough to stand alone when I must. But what a blessing each of us can be, if we try, to bless those around us. I testify that your power to stand alone, to live the gospel of Jesus Christ in hard circumstances, will be increased as you reach out to help others live it. And you will feel less alone as you do.

It's not hard to know what to do to help. People need to do some things that are simply said, but not easily done: First, they must exercise faith in the Lord Jesus Christ; second, repent, with a broken heart and contrite spirit; third, accept the ordinances of the gospel of Jesus Christ; and, fourth, gain the Holy Ghost as a constant companion. And you know, and I testify to you, that from these simple things will come in time the mighty change, and with that, the peace in this life and the hope of eternal life in the world to come will follow.

Let's begin with helping people to build faith: What could you do to make it more likely that someone you associate with will exercise faith in the Lord Jesus Christ? Example is one way. And, it is example that has had the most powerful effect in encouraging me to exercise faith. You and I have seen great faith. You've seen young people choose to serve missions when neither family nor circumstance made that easy. You may have served with one as a companion. You've seen a child, late on a fast day, watch intently as dinner is prepared. And then it dawned on you that they had fasted, twenty-four hours, because they loved the Savior, without either being spoken to or saying a word about it themselves. You've seen parents at the funeral of their child, tears streaming down their faces, thanking you for being so thoughtful to come. And they may have whispered to you, "Oh, we're fine. We know we will all be together again." You remember their smiles as much as their words, and you felt their faith.

You can be an example that will make it more likely that those near you will decide to exercise faith in the Lord Jesus Christ. There is at least one simple way to choose what you will do. And, by the way, you don't have to plan to be observed. You don't start with the idea of putting on a performance. Just start this way: Ask yourself this question, "What would the Savior have me do that I have been putting off because it seemed hard?" You won't have any trouble thinking of more than one. It doesn't have to seem hard to anybody else, just to you. Then, choose one from your list and do it. You might even try not to be observed. People who live and work with you notice more than you think. And they are more likely to exercise faith when they see your faith in Jesus Christ by your doing what for you took sacrifice.

Ask yourself this question, "What would the Savior have me do that I have been putting off because it seemed hard?" You won't have any trouble thinking of more than one. It doesn't have to seem hard to anybody else, just to you. Then, choose one from your list and do it.

You will also at times want to bear testimony of the Savior in words. That can build faith. Although you will do that in your own way as you are prompted, I can tell you what has helped me most. My heart seems to feel faith when the person speaking expresses both conviction and love. The conviction doesn't seem to come with the emotion in the voice as much as from the way I have seen the person behave. So your example may mean more than your words in conveying conviction. But, since my heart needs to be drawn toward the Savior, you help me most when your testimony includes words that tell me what you know about how the Savior loves you and loves me. That draws me to Him, and that's what I must feel to have faith enough to want to repent and to feel I will be forgiven.

You can be sure of this: When the person begins to feel real faith in Jesus Christ, they will begin to feel sorrow for sin. You can't make another person repent, but you can make it easier for them to want a repentant heart. The people who have helped me most have been those who asked my forgiveness as if it mattered to them and have forgiven me easily when I have offended. I've noticed, as perhaps you have, that such help most often comes from children. Aren't you softened when you see a child forgive so easily? Or when one says to you, with a catch in her voice, "I'm sorry, Daddy. Will you forgive me?"

I suppose that act of a little child works so powerfully on me because it makes me want to be like them—clean. And just that thought starts the inner review which so often leads to our asking forgiveness, both from those we have wronged and from God.

For most of us, that forgiveness needs to come often, for things we hope are small and that we catch early. That forgiveness is hard enough to seek, from others and from God. But when someone who is close to you begins to feel the desire to repent of larger, more serious sins, there is something else you can do to help. You have to start early, long before the need for forgiveness is felt.

It comes from this simple fact: Forgiveness for serious offenses requires both the forgiveness of the Lord and of the Lord's servants in His Church, who He calls "judges in Israel." You remember how those servants were instructed to deal with repentance in Mosiah:

"Therefore I say unto you, Go; and whosoever transgresseth against me, him shall ye judge according to the sins which he has committed; and if he confess his sins before thee and me, and repenteth in the sincerity of his heart, him shall ye forgive, and I will forgive him also.

"Yea, and as often as my people repent will I forgive them their trespasses against me" (Mosiah 26:29–30).

From that, you can see what you could start to do. And sooner is better. You could look for some evidence today that confirms your testimony that your bishop, your stake president, or some other of God's servants in the Church is inspired. And you could find a moment to share that with someone close to you. Do it over a long period of time, and I will tell you how that may be the key to peace someday for the person who hears you say those words.

They will always find it hard, even when they have faith and want so much to be free of the weight of serious sin, to go to a bishop, an ordinary person, to confess and to ask for forgiveness. It may be even harder to accept a decision a bishop or stake president may have to make by revelation to take away a privilege, or even membership in the Church, to help the person you love gain forgiveness and then find peace. If you speak early and often of your faith in the office and callings of God's servants, preferably ones you know well, and of your honest confidence in their inspiration, you will someday make a great difference. The person you blessed in that way will be more likely to make the choice for repentance and the remission of sins.

You know what comes next in the simple description of the path to God and to peace: baptism. For someone not yet baptized, or for someone who has lost their membership, that ordinance is necessary to have the Atonement work to bring the mighty change in a heart. But even someone in the Church will need to bring the effects of that baptism into their lives frequently. You may think of more ways than I can suggest to help, but I can give you two, offered to me by those around me. These may seem to you common things to do. But they can have an uncommon effect.

People around me have shown me by what they do how much

they honor and value covenants. Others have had that blessing, too. I remember hearing President Ezra Taft Benson tell of watching his mother press carefully her temple clothing, and of watching his parents pull out of their yard for the trip to the Logan Temple. I'm not sure how much his parents had to say about the value of a temple covenant. You don't have to say much to make it more likely that people around you will so treasure covenants to feel the remission of sins God promises by our keeping them.

You could show the value you place on the baptismal covenant by how regularly and carefully you renew it. You could be there, whatever your schedule and whatever your pressures, to partake of the sacrament when it is offered to you.

You could show the value you place on the baptismal covenant by how regularly and carefully you renew it. You could be there, whatever your schedule and whatever your pressures, to partake of the sacrament when it is offered to you. Each week, you do what the Lord commanded in the fifty-ninth section of the Doctrine and Covenants, the ninth verse: "And that thou mayest more fully keep thyself unspotted from the world, thou shalt go to the house of prayer and offer up thy sacraments upon my holy day."

And then, in verse 12, He goes on to say: "But remember that on this, the Lord's day, thou shalt offer thine oblations and thy sacraments unto the Most High, confessing thy sins unto thy brethren, and before the Lord."

The sacramental prayers were dictated by the Lord himself to keep us reminded of the gospel covenants we have made. Your being there to do that every Sabbath will make a difference for those close to you. And there is another way you could show that you value them. Here is what Alma said you promised as you made the baptismal covenant:

"Yea, and are willing to mourn with those that mourn; yea, and comfort those that stand in need of comfort, and to stand as witnesses of God at all times and in all things, and in all places that ye may be in, even until death, that ye may be redeemed of God, and be numbered with those of the first resurrection, that ye may have eternal life" (Mosiah 18:9).

Many of you, and some in my family, have shown me what believing and honoring that covenant can mean. You have shoveled coal out of one basement and into another for someone else, built homes for the homeless, fixed a rusted and broken dryer in the apartment of a single mother, tutored little children, and on and on—giving comfort to those who needed it, as you covenanted you would, and doing it when I could not see how you could possibly fit one more thing into hectic schedules. And, oh, how you have helped me by carrying a Book of Mormon every time you traveled, and then telling me with excitement of how a book was accepted. Because of you, I find myself trying harder to stand as a witness at all times and in all things and in all places that I may be in.

Now, listen to the end of that invitation to the covenant of baptism. Listen to what God promises to those who honor the covenant:

"Now I say unto you, if this be the desire of your hearts, what have you against being baptized in the name of the Lord, as a witness before him that ye have entered into a covenant with him, that ye will serve him and keep his commandments, that he may pour out his Spirit more abundantly upon you?" (Mosiah 18:10).

You know that the change and the peace we seek comes only

under the influence of the Holy Ghost. Remember how that wonderful process goes, because it tells you something about how to help others. You remember it was described this way in Moroni:

"And the remission of sins bringeth meekness, and lowliness of heart; and because of meekness and lowliness of heart cometh the visitation of the Holy Ghost, which Comforter filleth with hope and perfect love" (Moroni 8:26).

Think of that—the effect of feeling forgiveness is to feel meek and lowly. And that's what then allows you to have the Holy Ghost with you. You not only need to be meek and

> *The effect of feeling forgiveness is to feel meek and lowly. And that's what then allows you to have the Holy Ghost with you. You not only need to be meek and lowly to receive the Holy Ghost, but that is part of the effect He has on you when He visits.*

lowly to receive the Holy Ghost, but that is part of the effect He has on you when He visits. A passage from Galatians suggests what you might do to help someone welcome the Holy Ghost into their lives. It is a description of what having the Holy Ghost as your companion brings:

"But the fruit of the Spirit is love, joy, peace, longsuffering, gentleness, goodness, faith,

"Meekness, temperance: against such there is no law.

"And they that are Christ's have crucified the flesh with the affections and lusts.

"If we live in the Spirit, let us also walk in the Spirit.

"Let us not be desirous of vain glory, provoking one another, envying one another" (Galatians 5:22–26).

I've seen and felt how the people around me have helped me welcome the Holy Ghost more into my life. When I fish for vainglory in the form of a compliment for the sake of a compliment, I don't get much response at my house. Even when I act to provoke, they don't provoke back. And I never feel or see envy, at least from those closest to me. I don't know how conscious all that is. It may just be that they know, as you do, that when I am meek and lowly and quiet, I will more likely receive the Holy Ghost. And they love me enough to want that for me.

You might consider one other thing you could do to help those around you have the Holy Ghost as a companion. I don't know what pictures you have hanging on walls in your room. Nor do I know what music you play or what magazines you have around for others to see and read. But I've been blessed with people around me who seem to make those choices, again perhaps unconsciously, as if they wanted all the sights and sounds to help me feel, and keep feeling, love, joy, peace, long-suffering, gentleness, goodness, faith, meekness, and temperance. That doesn't make my home as dull a place as you might think. And I have felt and feel the Holy Ghost more often because of the music, and pictures, and words on a printed page, chosen by people around me. You could help someone that way, too. And you could start tonight.

Now, you will think of more ways than I have suggested to help those around you exercise faith, repent, make and keep covenants, and welcome the Holy Ghost. But it's important to be realistic about what to expect the results will be when you do.

You may be rejected. You may even meet anger. Now, you might well ask, "Wait a minute. You told me that I could bring peace, and instead I get war coming back at me. How can that be?"

First, don't feel picked on, because we've all had that happen. I have a memory of watching my little boys kick each other as they lay before me on the floor during our family night as I taught a lesson on peace in the family. In fact, that topic would bring it on. They heard me, they understood me, and yet they had been kicking for a long time before I started preaching. Now, years later, they reach across the world to help each other. But the change takes time. So be patient and persistent.

There are techniques for bringing quick, brief periods of peace in families as there are in cities and among nations. I recommend whatever of those techniques work and

I have felt and feel the Holy Ghost more often because of the music, and pictures, and words on a printed page, chosen by people around me. You could help someone that way, too.

do not interfere with the process of change that will give us peace in this life and eternal life in the world to come. But the change we need, the big and permanent change we need, takes some time. You can feel the patience you need by listening to this description given by Alma. It gives you a sense of the magnitude of the change that can come from the simple, small things we have talked about. You need to remember both how simple are the things to do and yet how great the change that is promised. I testify to you now this is true.

"And the Lord said unto me: Marvel not that all mankind, yea, men and women, all nations, kindreds, tongues and people, must be born again; yea, born of God, changed from their carnal and fallen state, to a state of righteousness, being redeemed of God, becoming his sons and daughters;

"And thus they become new creatures; and unless they do

this, they can in nowise inherit the kingdom of God" (Mosiah 27:25–26).

You would expect that will take some time and effort. And you would expect some setbacks along the way. For one thing, not all hatred comes from sin. Some of it is passed on to us by tradition. You remember what Jacob told the Nephites who were falling into sin. He told them that the Lamanites were more righteous than they were. And he said that the Lamanites hated only because of the traditions handed down to them. Habits of hatred may yield slowly, even to the power of the gospel.

But let me give you some encouragement that is certain. First, however much turmoil and violence you have had to live with, your spiritual longings, which come from the Father of your spirit, are for peace. However tough and hardened you have become, perhaps just to survive, what you really want is a heart softened by the gospel. And that change of heart in the people close to you will bring peace to them and with them.

And as you offer that help in living the gospel of Jesus Christ, that same gospel is working on you. You come unto Christ and become more like Him as you invite others to come unto Christ. When you become a peacemaker by offering the gospel of Jesus Christ, you also change by that same power. That may help you understand a scripture which is part of the promise made to you. The Savior has always made this promise to His disciples. You can hear it again in 3 Nephi. He said it the same way, in the same words, in His mortal ministry in Jerusalem: "And blessed are all the peacemakers, for they shall be called the children of God" (3 Nephi 12:9).

When I read that as a boy, I wondered about the promise. You remember that He promised the meek that they would inherit the earth and that the pure in heart would see God. It didn't sound like anything very glorious to be promised that you would be called the children of God for being a peacemaker. But you and I see now that the promise is both glorious and sure. Those who will have eternal life are the children of God. And the childlike heart which goes with that will come to you as you offer peace to the hearts of those around you.

That leads to one more encouragement which may help you. You may well doubt that you can have much effect on the people around you. But you will have help. You have been given, as you were given the gospel, the promise of help as you reach out to help. The Lord made a promise to His twelve disciples whom He chose among the people in the Americas, after His resurrection. He told them their role and gave them a promise: "Ye are my disciples; and ye are a light unto this people" (3 Nephi 15:12).

I testify that God knows you, that it is not by chance that you have found the gospel of Jesus Christ and His restored Church. He cares about those around you, and He loves you. You are His disciple, and that makes you a light to this people. When you act with faith to offer the gospel and peace to those around you, the light that will come to them will be more than your example and more than your words. They will feel the light of the Savior, and it will have drawn them to Him. You will have pointed the way President Taylor said to go. You remember his direction: "Peace is the gift of God. Do you want peace? Go to God. Do you want peace in your families? Go to God."

I testify to you that God lives, Jesus is the Christ. I testify that through the Prophet Joseph and each of the prophets who have followed him has come the power to offer ordinances that, if honored, lead to mighty change, to peace in this life, and eternal life in the world to come. I pray that you will offer peace, and so as peacemakers become the children of God.

FAITH AND KEYS

In a chapel far from Salt Lake City, in a place where a member of the Quorum of the Twelve rarely goes, a father approached me. He led his young son by the hand. As they reached me, he looked down at the boy, called him by name, and said, nodding his head towards me, "This is an Apostle." I could tell by the sound of the father's voice that he was hoping his son would feel more than that he was meeting a dignified visitor. He hoped that his son would feel a conviction that priesthood keys were on the earth in the Lord's Church. His son will need that conviction again and again. He will need it when he opens a letter from some future prophet he has never seen calling him to a mission. He will need it when he buries a child or a wife or a parent. He will need it for courage to follow direction to serve. He will need it for the comfort that comes from trusting a sealing power that binds forever.

Missionaries will invite investigators to meet a bishop or branch president today with the same intent. They hope that the investigators will feel far more than that they have met a nice man or even a great man. They will be praying that the investigators will feel a conviction that this apparently ordinary man holds priesthood keys in the Lord's Church. The investigators will need that conviction when they go into the waters of baptism. They will need it when they pay tithing. They will need that conviction when the bishop is inspired to give them a calling. They will need it when they see him presiding in the sacrament meeting and when he nourishes them by teaching the gospel.

And so missionaries and fathers, and all of us who serve others in the true Church, want to help those we love gain a lasting testimony that the keys of the priesthood are held by the Lord's servants in His Church. It will help to recognize some things. First, God is persistent and generous in offering the blessings of priesthood power to His children. Second, His children must choose for themselves to qualify for and receive those blessings. And third, Satan, the enemy of righteousness, has from the beginning tried to undermine the faith necessary to receive the blessings made possible by priesthood power.

I learned about those realities from a wise teacher more than thirty years ago. I spoke in an ancient theater in Ephesus. Bright sunlight flooded the ground where the Apostle Paul had stood to preach. My topic was Paul, the Apostle called of God.

The audience was hundreds of Latter-day Saints. They were arranged on the rows of stone benches the Ephesians sat upon more than a millennium before. Among them were two living Apostles, Elder Mark E. Petersen and Elder James E. Faust.

As you can imagine, I had prepared carefully. I had read the Acts of the Apostles and the Epistles, both those of Paul and his fellow Apostles. I had read and pondered Paul's Epistle to the Ephesians.

I tried my best to honor Paul and his office. After the talk, a number of people said kind things. Both of the living Apostles were generous in their comments. But later, Elder Faust took me aside and, with a smile and with softness in his voice, said, "That was a good talk. But you left out the most important thing you could have said."

I asked him what that was. Weeks later he consented to tell me. His answer has been teaching me ever since.

He said that I could have told the people that if the Saints who heard Paul had possessed a testimony of the value and the power of the keys he held, perhaps the Apostles would not have had to be taken from the earth.

That sent me back to Paul's letter to the Ephesians. I could see that Paul wanted the people to feel the value of the chain of priesthood keys reaching from the Lord through His Apostles to them, the members of the Lord's Church. Paul was trying to build a testimony of those keys.

If the Saints who heard Paul had possessed a testimony of the value and the power of the keys he held, perhaps the Apostles would not have had to be taken from the earth.

Paul testified to the Ephesians that Christ was at the head of His Church. And he taught that the Savior built His Church on a foundation of apostles and prophets who hold all the keys of the priesthood.

Despite the clarity and the power of his teaching and his example, Paul knew that an apostasy would come. He knew that apostles and prophets would be taken from the earth. And he knew that they would, in some great, future day, be restored. He wrote of that time to the Ephesians, speaking of what the Lord would do: "That in the dispensation of the fulness of times he might gather together in one all things in Christ, both which are in heaven, and which are on earth; even in him" (Ephesians 1:10).

Paul looked forward to the ministry of the Prophet Joseph Smith, when the heavens would be opened again. It happened.

John the Baptist came and conferred on mortals the priesthood of Aaron and the keys of the ministering of angels and of baptism by immersion for the remission of sins.

Ancient apostles and prophets returned and conferred upon Joseph the keys they held in mortality. Mortal men were ordained to the holy apostleship in February of 1835. Priesthood keys were given to the Twelve Apostles in the latter part of March 1844.

The Prophet Joseph Smith knew that his death was imminent. He knew that the precious priesthood keys and the apostleship must not be and would not be lost again.

One of the Apostles, Wilford Woodruff, left us this account of what happened in Nauvoo as the Prophet spoke to the Twelve:

"On that occasion the Prophet Joseph rose up and said to us: 'Brethren, I have desired to live to see this temple built. I shall never live to see it, but you will. I have sealed upon your heads all the keys of the kingdom of God. I have sealed upon you every key, power, principle that the God of heaven has revealed to me. Now, no matter where I may go or what I may do, the kingdom rests upon you'" ("The Keys of the Kingdom," *Ensign*, April 2004, 30).

Every prophet that followed Joseph, from Brigham Young to Thomas S. Monson, has held and exercised those keys and has held the sacred apostleship.

But just as in the time of Paul, the power of those priesthood keys for us requires our faith. We have to know by inspiration that the priesthood keys are held by those who lead and serve us. That requires the witness of the Spirit.

And that depends upon our testimony that Jesus is the Christ and that He lives and leads His Church. We must also know for ourselves that the Lord restored His Church and the priesthood keys through the Prophet Joseph Smith. And we must have an assurance through the Holy Ghost, refreshed often, that those keys have been passed without interruption to the living prophet and that the Lord blesses and directs His people through the line of priesthood keys that reaches down through presidents of stakes and of districts and through bishops and branch presidents to us, wherever we are and no matter how far from the prophet and the Apostles.

That is not easy today. It was not easy in the days of Paul. It has always been hard to recognize in fallible human beings the authorized servants of God. Paul must have seemed an ordinary man to many. Joseph Smith's cheerful disposition was seen by some as not fitting their expectations for a prophet of God.

Satan will always work on the Saints of God to undermine their faith in priesthood keys. One way he does it is to point out the humanity of those who hold them.

Satan will always work on the Saints of God to undermine their faith in priesthood keys. One way he does it is to point out the humanity of those who hold them. He can in that way weaken our testimony and so cut us loose from the line of keys by which the Lord ties us to Him and can take us and our families home to Him and to our Heavenly Father.

Satan succeeded in undermining the testimony of men who had, with Joseph Smith, seen the heavens opened and heard the voices of angels. The evidence of their physical eyes and ears was not enough when they no longer could feel the testimony that the priesthood keys were still in place with Joseph.

The warning for us is plain. If we look for human frailty in humans, we will always find it. When we focus on finding the frailties of those who hold priesthood keys, we run risks for ourselves. When we speak or write to others of such frailties, we put them at risk.

We live in a world where finding fault in others seems to be the favorite blood sport. It has long been the basis of political campaign strategy. It is the theme of much television programming across the world. It sells newspapers. Whenever we meet anyone, our first, almost unconscious reaction may be to look for imperfections.

To keep ourselves grounded in the Lord's Church, we can and must train our eyes to recognize the power of the Lord in the service of those He has called. We must be worthy of the companionship of the Holy Ghost. And we need to pray for the Holy Ghost to help us know that men who lead us hold this power. For me, such prayers are most often answered when I am fully engaged in the Lord's service myself.

It happened in the aftermath of a disaster. A dam in Idaho broke on a June day. A wall of water struck the communities below it. Thousands of people, mostly Latter-day Saints, fled their homes to go to safety.

I was there as the people faced the terrible task of recovery. I saw the stake president gather his bishops to lead the people. We were cut off in those first days from any supervision from outside. I was in the meeting of local leaders when a director from the federal disaster agency arrived.

He tried to take over the meeting. With great force he began to list the things that he said needed to be done. As he read aloud each item, the stake president, who was sitting near him, said quietly, "We've already done that." After that went on for five or ten minutes, the federal official grew silent and sat down. He listened quietly as the stake president took reports from the bishops and gave directions.

For the meeting the next day, the federal disaster official arrived early. He sat toward the back. The stake president began the meeting. He took more reports, and he gave instructions. After a few minutes, the federal official, who had come with all the authority and resources of his great agency, said, "President Ricks, what would you like us to do?"

He recognized power. I saw more. I recognized the evidence of keys and the faith that unlocks their power.

I learned then as I have since how the stakes of Zion become places of safety. They become like a great family, united, caring for each other. It comes by simple faith.

With continual changes comes a great opportunity. We can act to qualify for the revelation that allows us to know that the keys are being passed by God from one person to another.

By faith they are baptized and receive the Holy Ghost. As they continue to keep the commandments, that gift becomes constant. They can recognize spiritual things. It becomes easier to see the power of God working through the common people God calls to serve and lead them. Hearts are softened. Strangers become fellow citizens in the Lord's kingdom, united in loving bonds.

That happy condition will not last without a constant renewal of faith. The bishop we love will be released, as will the stake president. The Apostles we followed in faith will be taken home to the God who called them.

With those continual changes comes a great opportunity. We

can act to qualify for the revelation that allows us to know that the keys are being passed by God from one person to another. We can seek to have that experience again and again. And we must, in order to receive the blessings God has for us and wants us to offer to others.

The answer to your prayer is not likely to be as dramatic as it was when some saw Brigham Young, as he spoke, take on the appearance of the martyred Prophet Joseph. But it can be as sure. And with that spiritual assurance will come peace and power. You will know again that this is the Lord's true and living Church, that He leads it through His ordained servants, and that He cares about us.

If enough of us exercise that faith and receive those assurances, God will lift up those who lead us and so bless our lives and our families. We will become what Paul so wanted for those he served: "built upon the foundation of the apostles and prophets, Jesus Christ himself being the chief corner stone" (Ephesians 2:20).

O Remember, Remember

When our children were very small, I started to write down a few things about what happened every day. Let me tell you how that got started. I came home late from a Church assignment. It was after dark. My father-in-law, who lived near us, surprised me as I walked toward the front door of my house. He was carrying a load of pipes over his shoulder, walking very fast and dressed in his work clothes. I knew that he had been building a system to pump water from a stream below us up to our property.

He smiled, spoke softly, and then rushed past me into the darkness to go on with his work. I took a few steps toward the house, thinking of what he was doing for us, and just as I got to the door, I heard in my mind—not in my own voice—these words: "I'm not giving you these experiences for yourself. Write them down."

I went inside. I didn't go to bed. Although I was tired, I took out some paper and began to write. And as I did, I understood the message I had heard in my mind. I was supposed to record for my children to read, someday in the future, how I had seen the hand of God blessing our family. Grandpa didn't have to do what he was doing for us. He could have had someone else do it or not have done it at all. But he was serving us, his family, in the way covenant disciples of Jesus Christ always do. I knew that was true. And so I wrote it down, so that my children could have the memory some-day when they would need it.

I wrote down a few lines every day for years. I never missed a day no matter how tired I was or how early I would have to start the next day. Before I would write, I would ponder this question: "Have I seen the hand of God reaching out to touch us or our children or our family today?" As I kept at it, something began to happen. As I would cast my mind over the day, I would see evidence of what God had done for one of us that I had not recognized in the busy moments of the day. As that happened, and it happened often, I realized that trying to remember had allowed God to show me what He had done.

More than gratitude be-gan to grow in my heart. Testi-mony grew. I became ever more certain that our Heavenly Father hears and answers prayers. I felt more gratitude

I wrote down a few lines every day for years. I never missed a day no matter how tired I was or how early I would have to start the next day. As I would cast my mind over the day, I would see evidence of what God had done for one of us that I had not recognized in the busy moments of the day. As that happened, and it happened often, I realized that trying to remember had allowed God to show me what He had done.

for the softening and refining that come because of the Atonement of the Savior Jesus Christ. And I grew more confident that the Holy Ghost can bring all things to our remembrance—even things we did not notice or pay attention to when they happened.

The years have gone by. My boys are grown men. And now and then one of them will surprise me by saying, "Dad, I was reading in my copy of the journal about when . . ." and then he will tell me about how reading of what happened long ago helped him notice something God had done in his day.

My point is to urge you to find ways to recognize and remember God's kindness. It will build our testimonies. You may not keep a journal. You may not share whatever record you keep with those you love and serve. But you and they will be blessed as you remember what the Lord has done. You remember that song we sometimes sing: "Count your many blessings; name them one by one, And it will surprise you what the Lord has done" (Johnson Oatman, Jr., "Count Your Blessings," *Hymns*, no. 241).

It won't be easy to remember. Living as we do with a veil over our eyes, we cannot remember what it was like to be with our Heavenly Father and His Beloved Son, Jesus Christ, in the premortal world; nor can we see with our physical eyes or with reason alone the hand of God in our lives. Seeing such things takes the Holy Ghost. And it is not easy to be worthy of the Holy Ghost's companionship in a wicked world.

That is why forgetting God has been such a persistent problem among His children since the world began. Think of the times of Moses, when God provided manna and in miraculous and visible ways led and protected His children. Still, the prophet warned the people who had been so blessed, as prophets always have warned and always will: "Take heed to thyself, and keep thy soul diligently, lest thou forget the things which thine eyes have seen, and lest they depart from thy heart all the days of thy life" (Deuteronomy 4:9).

And the challenge to remember has always been the hardest for those who are blessed abundantly. Those who are faithful to God are protected and prospered. That comes as the result of serving

God and keeping His commandments. But with those blessings comes the temptation to forget their source. It is easy to begin to feel the blessings were granted not by a loving God on whom we depend but by our own powers. The prophets have repeated this lament over and over:

"And thus we can behold how false, and also the unsteadiness of the hearts of the children of men; yea, we can see that the Lord in his great infinite goodness doth bless and prosper those who put their trust in him.

"Yea, and we may see at the very time when he doth prosper his people, yea, in the increase of their fields, their flocks and their herds, and in gold, and in silver, and in all manner of precious things of every kind and art; sparing their lives, and delivering them out of the hands of their enemies; softening the hearts of their enemies that they should not declare wars against them; yea, and in fine, doing all things for the welfare and happiness of his people; yea, then is the time that they do harden their hearts, and do forget the Lord their God, and do trample under their feet the Holy One—yea, and this because of their ease, and their exceedingly great prosperity."

And the prophet goes on to say: "Yea, how quick to be lifted up in pride; yea, how quick to boast, and do all manner of that which is iniquity; and how slow are they to remember the Lord their God, and to give ear unto his counsels, yea, how slow to walk in wisdom's paths!" (Helaman 12:1–2, 5).

Sadly, prosperity is not the only reason people forget God. It can also be hard to remember Him when our lives go badly. When we struggle, as so many do, in grinding poverty or when our enemies prevail against us or when sickness is not healed, the enemy of our souls can send his evil message that there is no God or that if He exists He does not care about us. Then it can be hard for the

Holy Ghost to bring to our remembrance the lifetime of blessings the Lord has given us from our infancy and in the midst of our distress.

There is a simple cure for the terrible malady of forgetting God, His blessings, and His messages to us. Jesus Christ promised it to His disciples when He was about to be crucified, resurrected, and then taken away from them to ascend in glory to His Father. They were concerned to know how they would be able to endure when He was no longer with them.

Here is the promise. It was fulfilled for them then. It can be fulfilled for all of us now:

"These things have I spoken unto you, being yet present with you.

"But the Comforter, which is the Holy Ghost, whom the Father will send in my name, he shall teach you all things, and bring all things to your remembrance, whatsoever I have said unto you" (John 14:25–26).

The key to the remembering that brings and maintains testimony is receiving the Holy Ghost as a companion. It is the Holy Ghost who helps us see what God has done for us. It is the Holy Ghost who can help those we serve to see what God has done for them.

Heavenly Father has given a simple pattern for us to receive the Holy Ghost not once but continually in the tumult of our daily lives. The pattern is repeated in the sacramental prayer: We promise that we will always remember the Savior. We promise to take His name upon us. We promise to keep His commandments. And we are promised that if we do that, we will have His Spirit to be with us (see Doctrine and Covenants 20:77, 79). Those promises work together in a wonderful way to strengthen our testimonies and in time, through the Atonement, to change our natures as we keep our part of the promise.

It is the Holy Ghost who testifies that Jesus Christ is the Beloved Son of a Heavenly Father who loves us and wants us to have eternal life with Him in families. With even the beginning of that testimony, we feel a desire to serve Him and to keep His commandments. When we persist in doing that, we receive the gifts of the Holy Ghost to give us power in our service. We come to see the hand of God more clearly, so clearly that in time we not only remember Him, but we come to love Him and, through the power of the Atonement, become more like Him.

You might ask, "But how does this process get started in someone who knows nothing about God and claims no memory of spiritual experiences at all?" Everyone has had spiritual experiences that they may not have recognized. Every person, upon entering the world, is given the Spirit of Christ. Even before people receive the right to the gifts of the Holy Ghost, when they are confirmed as members of the Church, and even before the Holy Ghost confirms truth to them before baptism, they have spiritual experiences. The Spirit of Christ has already, from their childhood, invited them to do good and warned them against evil. They have memories of those experiences even if they have not recognized their source. That memory will come back to them as missionaries or we teach them the word of God and they hear it. They will remember the feeling of joy or sorrow when they are taught the truths of the gospel. And that memory of the Spirit of Christ will soften their hearts to allow the Holy Ghost to testify to them. That will lead them to keep commandments and want to take the name of the Savior upon them. And when they do, in the waters of baptism, and as they hear the words in confirmation "Receive the Holy Ghost" spoken by an authorized servant of God, the power to always remember God will be increased.

Each night, you might pray and ponder, asking the questions: "Did God send a message today that was just for me? Did I see His hand in my life or the lives of my children?"

Each night, you might pray and ponder, asking the questions: "Did God send a message today that was just for me? Did I see His hand in my life or the lives of my children?" I will do that. And then I will find a way to preserve that memory for the day that I, and those that I love, will need to remember how much God loves us and how much we need Him. I testify that He loves us and blesses us, more than most of us have yet recognized. I know that is true, and it brings me joy to remember Him.

RAISE THE BAR

Change is accelerating in the world around us. Some of that change is for the better. But much of the acceleration in the world is in troubles long prophesied for the last days. Each time you watch the evening news, you see stark evidence of that. You remember this scripture: "For behold, at that day shall he [meaning Satan] rage in the hearts of the children of men, and stir them up to anger against that which is good" (2 Nephi 28:20).

The Lord told us in the time of the Prophet Joseph that war would be poured out upon all nations. We see tragic fulfillment of that prophecy, bringing with it increased suffering to the innocent.

Giant earthquakes, and the tsunamis they have sent crashing into the coasts of the surrounding areas, are just the beginning and a part of what is to come. You remember the words from the Doctrine and Covenants, which now seem so accurate:

"And after your testimony cometh wrath and indignation upon the people.

"For after your testimony cometh the testimony of earthquakes, that shall cause groanings in the midst of her, and men shall fall upon the ground and shall not be able to stand.

"And also cometh the testimony of the voice of thunderings, and the voice of lightnings, and the voice of tempests, and the voice of the waves of the sea heaving themselves beyond their bounds.

"And all things shall be in commotion; and surely, men's hearts shall fail them; for fear shall come upon all people (Doctrine and Covenants 88:88–91).

Fear shall come upon all people. But you and I know that the Lord has prepared places of safety to which He is eager to guide us.

> *Fear shall come upon all people. But you and I know that the Lord has prepared places of safety to which He is eager to guide us.*

I think of that often. Consider, for example, two accounts I heard of God leading His children to safety on the coast of Thailand when a monstrous tsunami wave struck there in 2004.

One was of people who accepted His apparently routine invitation to a Church meeting on a Sunday. The meeting was called by ordinary men who hold the priesthood of God. The meeting place was on higher ground, away from the coast. The people who gathered with the Saints were spared from physical death, while the places on the coast where they would have been were destroyed. As they were spared physical death, they were being strengthened against spiritual temptation and the wave of eternal tragedy it will bring to those who are disobedient.

The other account I heard was related to me by a Latter-day Saint who was led to safety by the Holy Ghost. He checked into a hotel on the ocean front in Thailand the day before the wave struck. He walked out on the beach. He felt uneasy. He went back to his hotel determined to check out. The hotel staff, I think worried that he didn't like the hotel, pressed him for a reason. They only reluctantly agreed to his leaving. He moved to another hotel, away from the beach. It was on higher ground. Because of that, he not only survived but stayed to serve the survivors.

The Lord is anxious to lead us to the safety of higher ground, away from the path of physical and spiritual danger. His upward path will require us to climb. My mother used to say to me when I complained that things were hard, "If you are on the right path, it will always be uphill." And as the world becomes darker and more dangerous, we must keep climbing. It will be our choice whether or not to move up or to stay where we are. But the Lord will invite and guide us upward by the direction of the Holy Ghost, which He sends to His leaders and to His people who will receive it.

The Lord is anxious to lead us to the safety of higher ground, away from the path of physical and spiritual danger. His upward path will require us to climb. My mother used to say to me when I complained that things were hard, "If you are on the right path, it will always be uphill."

The mists of spiritual darkness will become more dense as we climb. They are described in the Book of Mormon this way: "And the mists of darkness are the temptations of the devil, which blindeth the eyes, and hardeneth the hearts of the children of men, and leadeth them away into broad roads, that they perish and are lost" (1 Nephi 12:17).

But the word of God will guide those who develop the capacity to receive it through the ministrations of the Holy Ghost. A clear light piercing the darkness will show the way to those who have taken the Holy Ghost as a trusted and constant traveling companion.

Most of us who are members of the restored Church have enough faith to want the Holy Ghost at times. That desire may be weak and intermittent, but it comes, usually when we are in trouble. For us to be led upward to safety in the times ahead, it must become steady and intense.

The problem for most human beings is that when things go well, we feel self-sufficient. You remember the warning:

"And others will he pacify, [again speaking of Satan] and lull them away into carnal security, that they will say: All is well in Zion; yea, Zion prospereth, all is well—and thus the devil cheateth their souls, and leadeth them away carefully down to hell" (2 Nephi 28:21).

And later comes the warning:

"Cursed is he that putteth his trust in man, or maketh flesh his arm, or shall hearken unto the precepts of men, save their precepts shall be given by the power of the Holy Ghost" (2 Nephi 28:31).

If you examine your own experience carefully and honestly, you will see that you tend to seek the Holy Ghost most fervently when you are humbled by difficult circumstances or life-changing decisions. Remember the time you faced the prospect of teaching the gospel as a missionary perhaps in a new language where you couldn't understand what people were saying and you couldn't put a sentence together. Or, remember a time you had to make choices that might lead you toward, or away from, marrying someone. Those moments probably brought a great desire for the faith and the capacity to get the help of the Holy Ghost.

But if we have to be in trouble to want the Holy Ghost as a constant companion, then to have that steady desire we will have to be in steady trouble. There has to be a better way.

Happily, there is. Now you will have to find your own. I'll tell you mine. There is one for me that works: I choose to remind myself about my experience with what prophets have said about the peace and happiness that comes with the visitation of the Holy Ghost. It has been true in my life. Wilford Woodruff described it this way:

"You may surround any man or woman with all the wealth and glory that the imagination of man can grasp, and are they satisfied? No. There is still an aching void. On the other hand, show me a beggar upon the streets, who has the Holy Ghost, whose mind is filled with that Spirit and power, and I will show you a person who has peace of mind, who possesses true riches, and those enjoyments that no man can obtain from any other source" (*Journal of Discourses,* 26 vols. [1854–1886], 2:199).

If we have to be in trouble to want the Holy Ghost as a constant companion, then to have that steady desire we will have to be in steady trouble. There has to be a better way.

That has been true for me. One of the ways I know that I'm feeling the influence of the Holy Ghost is that I feel a light and I am happy. When the Holy Ghost seems far from me, I feel a darkness and I am not happy. I have felt that ebb and flow of light and happiness in my life and so have you.

I like to feel of that light and I like to be happy. I don't have to wait for troubles and tests to make me want the help of the Holy Ghost. I can choose to remember what that companionship has been like, and whenever I do, I want that blessing again with my whole heart.

When we want the Holy Ghost and the peace of mind and enjoyment that comes with it, we know what to do. We plead with God for it in faith. It takes the prayer of faith to bring the companionship of the Holy Ghost. That faith has to be that God the Father, the Creator of all things, lives and wants us to have the Holy Ghost and wants to send us the Comforter. It takes faith that Jesus is the Christ and that He atoned for our sins and broke the bands of death. With that faith we approach our Father in reverence and with confidence that He will answer. With that faith we close our prayer in the name of Jesus Christ as His true disciples, confident that our deep repentance, our baptism by His servants, and our faithful service in His cause have purified us and made us clean and worthy of the blessing we seek, the companionship of the Holy Ghost.

I have found myself setting a higher standard for my prayers for the Holy Ghost to guide me because of the great examples of others. A favorite for me is in 3 Nephi. Jesus had chosen disciples who would need the Holy Ghost as their companion when He was gone. Their example lifts me every time I read it and could lift you: "And they did pray for that which they most desired; and they desired that the Holy Ghost should be given unto them" (3 Nephi 19:9). It helps me to plead with more desire and faith when I read again the answer to their prayer:

"The Holy Ghost did fall upon them, and they were filled with the Holy Ghost and with fire. And behold, they were encircled about as if it were by fire; and it came down from heaven, and the multitude did witness it, and did bear record" (3 Nephi 19:13–14).

My prayers to receive the help of the Holy Ghost have been strengthened by pondering the record of the scriptures. And so has been my ability to recognize the message which the Holy Ghost brings. The scriptures tell us why that is so. The scripture declares:

"Angels speak by the power of the Holy Ghost; wherefore, they speak the words of Christ. Wherefore, I said unto you, feast upon the words of Christ; for behold, the words of Christ will tell you all things what ye should do.

"Wherefore, now after I have spoken these words, if ye cannot understand them it will be because ye ask not, neither do ye knock; wherefore, ye are not brought into the light, but must perish in the dark.

"For behold, again I say unto you that if ye will enter in by the way, and receive the Holy Ghost, it will show unto you all things what ye should do" (2 Nephi 32:3–5).

When I read the words spoken by the Savior in the scriptures, I grow in my capacity to recognize inspiration from the Holy Ghost.

I have found that is true: the words of inspiration from the Holy Ghost are words the Savior used. When I read the words spoken by the Savior in the scriptures, I grow in my capacity to recognize inspiration from the Holy Ghost. For that reason my personal scriptures tend to wear out unevenly. I go most often to those places in the Book of Mormon, in the Doctrine and Covenants, and in the Bible where the Lord is speaking. By doing that I can better recognize the voice of the Spirit when the Savior's words echo easily in my mind.

Just as pondering the scriptures invites the companionship of the Holy Ghost, so does doing the things we have been told to do and doing them promptly. We are promised that the scriptures and the Holy Ghost will tell us all things that we should do. When we go and do what we have been told and do it the best we can, we qualify for more instructions of what to do. If we do not act, we will not receive further instructions. My hero in this is the prophet Nephi, described in the book of Helaman. He is my example for "Go and do."

"And behold, now it came to pass that when the Lord had spoken these words unto Nephi, he did stop and did not go unto his own house, but did return unto the multitudes who were scattered about upon the face of the land, and began to declare unto them the word of the Lord which had been spoken unto him, concerning their destruction if they did not repent" (Helaman 10:12).

His immediate obedience brought him the companionship of the Holy Ghost, just as it will for you and me. Here is the account:

"The power of God was with him, and they could not take him to cast him into prison, for he was taken by the Spirit and conveyed away out of the midst of them.

"And it came to pass that thus he did go forth in the Spirit, from multitude to multitude, declaring the word of God, even until he had declared it unto them all, or sent it forth among all the people" (Helaman 10:16–17).

Now, there is a wonderful way in which all the things about which we have spoken work together. Desire for the Holy Ghost leads us to the prayer of faith. Pondering the words of the Savior in the scriptures increases our capacity to recognize the voice of the Spirit. The Spirit and the words of Christ tell us all things that we must do. And as we do those things, we qualify for further inspiration by the Spirit. And, in time, that companionship of the Holy Ghost changes us. We feel the effects of the Atonement. Our desire for light increases, and so we pray with greater faith that our prayers will be answered. The scriptures open up to us more clearly, our power to obey becomes greater, and we are drawn ever upward, higher and higher, toward purity and happiness and eternal safety (see 3 Nephi 27:20; Alma 19:33; 3 Nephi 9:20).

Now, all this has some practical applications for each of us. One is that we can repent and be cleansed to qualify for the gift of the Holy Ghost. That makes us optimists. We can be forgiven and be worthy to receive the Holy Ghost. With that gift, things will work out. The Holy Ghost has a sanctifying influence. So, people can improve. Tomorrow will be better. We can have rising expectations.

You can set the bar for yourself a little higher and then a little higher, again and again.

For instance, you returned missionaries can set your goal not to maintain the spirituality you felt in the mission field, but to rise higher. That will take work and determination but you can do it. Other people did some of your work for you, which you must now do for yourself. For instance, the Church set the bar higher for the standard to become a full-time missionary. Your mission president urged and lifted you to higher standards. Now, it is your responsibility to set the bar higher for yourself, not once, but again and again.

Desire for the Holy Ghost leads us to the prayer of faith. Pondering the words of the Savior in the scriptures increases our capacity to recognize the voice of the Spirit. The Spirit and the words of Christ tell us all things that we must do. And as we do those things, we qualify for further inspiration by the Spirit.

That is true for all of us, not just for those who have been missionaries. In my ten years on the faculty at Stanford, I was blessed never to teach the same course twice. I moved from field to field and changed every course I taught, every time. I remember the nights when I was still working when the dawn came. I remember the adrenaline pumping when I stood to face students with material as new to me as it was to them. I know that I got help from the Holy Ghost.

As the challenges around us increase, we must commit to do more to qualify for the companionship of the Holy Ghost. Casual prayer won't be enough. Reading a few verses of the scripture won't be enough. Doing the minimum of what the Lord asks of us won't be enough. Hoping that we will have the Atonement work in our lives and that we will perhaps sometimes feel the influence of the Holy Ghost won't be enough. And one great burst of effort won't be enough.

> As the challenges around us increase, we must commit to do more to qualify for the companionship of the Holy Ghost. Casual prayer won't be enough. Reading a few verses of the scripture won't be enough. Doing the minimum of what the Lord asks of us won't be enough.

Only a steady, ever-increasing effort will allow the Lord to take us to higher ground. I know what some of you are tempted to think: "I'll have to be careful not to set the bar for myself too high. I wouldn't want to fail and be disappointed."

I did a little high-jumping over a bar in high school and in college. I know what it is like to be running toward the bar and see that it is higher than when you jumped last and that you are now looking way up at the bar. Some of you have been high-jumpers so that you know that it is very different when you come toward it so that you can look over it. I know what happens when you look up at that bar. You think, "That bar is over my head. Is it physically possible to put my whole body over a bar above my head?" As I look back, remember I was a physics student, I realized that I must have decided that some law of physics limited me. Well, the laws of physics did apply, but the limits were more in my mind than in reality. When I now see junior high school students, some of them girls, jumping higher than my best, I wish that I were young again. I'd set my expectations higher. More was possible than I thought, and more is possible spiritually for you and for me. And more is necessary. Set the bar a little higher for yourself. And then set it a little higher. In spiritual things you have a heavenly power lifting you beyond where you are now. The Lord promises that unending rise in his own voice in the Doctrine and Covenants: "That which is of God is light; and he that receiveth light, and continueth in God, receiveth more light; and that light groweth brighter and brighter until the perfect day" (Doctrine and Covenants 50:24).

You can set the bar higher for yourself to get more power of faith to pray for the gift of the Holy Ghost. You can set it higher for yourself to have the scriptures opened so that you will come to know the Savior's voice. You can set it higher for yourself to be obedient in the things He asks of you. And you can set the bar higher in your expectation for peace in this life and your hope, even your assurance of eternal life in the world to come. You can set your expectations for yourself a little higher and then a little higher, with confidence that a loving Heavenly Father and His Beloved Son will send you the Holy Ghost and lift you higher and higher, toward Them.

INDEX

INDEX

Index